choosing
compassion

also by Anam Thubten

Embracing Each Moment:
A Guide to the Awakened Life

The Magic of Awareness

No Self, No Problem:
Awakening to Our True Nature

choosing
compassion

how to be
of benefit in a world
that needs our love

ANAM THUBTEN

Shambhala

BOULDER · 2019

Shambhala Publications, Inc.
4720 Walnut Street
Boulder, Colorado 80301
www.shambhala.com

9 8 7 6 5 4 3 2 1

First Edition
Printed in the United States of America

♾ This edition is printed on acid-free paper that meets the
American National Standards Institute Z39.48 Standard.
♻ This book is printed on 30% postconsumer recycled paper.
For more information please visit www.shambhala.com.
Shambhala Publications is distributed worldwide by
Penguin Random House, Inc., and its subsidiaries.

Designed by Kate Huber-Parker

Library of Congress Cataloging-in-Publication Data
Names: Thubten, Anam, author.
Title: Choosing compassion: how to be of benefit
in a world that needs our love / Anam Thubten.
Description: First edition. | Shambhala: Shambhala, 2019.
Identifiers: LCCN 2018049214 | ISBN 9781611807271 (pbk.: alk. paper)
Subjects: LCSH: Compassion—Religious aspects—Buddhism.
Classification: LCC BQ4360 .T48 2019 | DDC 294.3/5677—dc23
LC record available at https://lccn.loc.gov/2018049214

contents

preface

Many of us have a strong habit of getting bogged down by the exterior aspects of life: politics, news, work, relationships, and finances to name a few. This can cause us to feel that we're stuck with a life that is devoid of meaning and joy. Not only that, but this can bind us to a limiting version of reality, and we suffer as its consequence. The interior world of mind and heart are neglected when our whole focus is given to external values. Therefore, spiritual teachings often invite us to pause and turn our attention inward to cultivate the wealth of wisdom, love, and compassion. My hope is that *Choosing Compassion* will do this very job for whomever comes across it.

Books have their own life and mission just like people. They go to places where an author has never been and reach people an author has never met, hopefully giving them the inspiration they might be looking for. This is not my first book. During my lecture tours, now and then a new face will show up with one of my books filled with marks, and the person will tell me it helped them. Knowing that my work is benefiting someone out there has inspired me to teach and write more. My books also have been wonderful bridges between many people around the world and me. As long as my books are helping people, it feels worthwhile to continue to write them. As individuals, we constantly change, along with our culture.

New ideas and refreshing language that address our problems and solutions are very much needed.

We live in a very interesting time in the history of humankind, due to rapid changes on all levels. The systems that used to make sense are collapsing. We are anxious about a very uncertain future as ecological crises hit us stronger and stronger each year. Yet, there is a sanctuary where we can take refuge. It is not out there in the world; it is in the love and wisdom that can be found within our heart. And so, in addition to, and perhaps because of, the challenges that are being presented to us collectively and individually, this is also a potent time for our inner growth. There is usually an upside to the experiences we go through in this life, regardless of whether we can see this upside immediately or not.

Choosing Compassion is based on my talks given at our temple in Point Richmond, California: a quaint historical town with magical sunsets and views of the famous Golden Gate Bridge that can get anyone drunk with bliss. Almost every other week, people come to the temple and we meditate together as a community, followed by a talk. Much of the audience already has a strong foundation in various wisdom traditions. In many ways, this book doesn't just belong to me; it also belongs to all these wonderful people. It only came into being because they inspired me to teach.

Let me take this as an opportunity to express my gratitude to everyone who worked to make this book available. It has taken the efforts of many, who have helped by recording talks, transcribing them, editing them, and more. I am especially grateful to Sharon Roe, who continuously helps my books take form thanks to her contagious enthusiasm and sharp editing.

*choosing
compassion*

I

circle of love

It is important to bring hearts full of compassion and love into our daily spiritual practice. Without that our practice is incomplete. There is a beautiful phrase designed to help us open our hearts: "May all beings be free from suffering and the cause of suffering." Tibetans have been reciting this phrase for centuries. It could be turned into a lyric for an international anthem, but we're not yet there. The world needs more unity and mutual understanding before we're ready to create such an anthem that carries this good message. While invoking this prayer we can imagine everybody in the world and hold them in our hearts with love and compassion. First, we can visualize our family and friends, and then those with whom we have difficulties. Finally, we can visualize all of humanity as one giant family. When we feel this deep desire for all beings to be free from suffering, it is quite easy to dissolve the defenses that close our hearts.

Our ego has layers and layers of defense. These defenses include fear, anger, hatred, and excessive self-cherishing. However, when we begin to feel the ocean of suffering that pervades our world, we also begin to notice our own suffering. Suffering is one of the most important topics in Buddhist traditions, and sometimes that is very unpopular. Many people don't want to hear anything about suffering, even though there is an ocean of suffering in our world. When our hearts are not open, we don't feel the suffering of others. Our defenses, those aspects of our personality that shield our own hearts from pain, prevent us from feeling the suffering of others. Sometimes we justify the causes and reasons for their suffering. We may even blame them. Our defenses prevent us from feeling the pain of others, and the omnipresent suffering in our world becomes quite unrelated to our everyday life as long as we ourselves are doing okay. We may not feel what is happening in our own hearts and in our minds because we are using many strategies to close down our awareness of pain both in others and in ourselves. This form of unawareness is quite prevalent in our society today. Many spiritual masters have been calling on us to wake up from such unawareness and not only feel love toward others but also act on it through kindness, generosity, and sacrifice. Thomas Merton beautifully summarized their messages when he said that we should live not for ourselves but for others. There are many in this world who embody this message. Many of these people are not recognized as saints or heroes. They are unsung heroes and heroines. The irony is that we have created specific individuals as icons of love and altruism while many ordinary people demonstrate these virtues in everyday life. However, maybe we need to create icons in order to inspire the public to practice these virtues.

One time, I was watching the animated Disney movie *Wall-E*, which illustrates the themes of feeling numb to our own suffering and that of others. In the film, the earth was completely destroyed. Everybody jumped aboard a giant spaceship in order to be saved. People didn't have to work on the spaceship. All they did, twenty-four hours a day, was sit on a chair and relax. They could order whatever they wanted to eat and drink, and everything they ordered arrived immediately. They pushed a button and Coca-Cola appeared directly in front of them. Then they pushed another button and french fries popped up. They watched sports and other entertaining programs all day long and didn't move. They just sat on their chair all day eating, drinking, and laughing. Often, they sat next to their spouse and their children or other family members. Sometimes they touched each other but when they did, they didn't feel anything because they had become desensitized. Outwardly they all were very happy. They loved this relaxing lifestyle, but eventually they became so lazy they couldn't move around very easily.

This movie had a message. It showed what Buddhists calls *all-pervasive unawareness*. This is a state where we close our heart so we don't have to feel our own suffering, and of course, we don't have to feel the suffering of others either. Ancient adepts remind us that we won't evolve personally—and humanity as a whole won't evolve either—until we start cultivating love and compassion for ourselves and all others. Our circle of love and compassion can continue to grow and expand. Our heart can grow forever. It has no limits. As an example, consider the Buddha. He showed limitless love and compassion to people from all walks of life, regardless of their social status or caste. His compassion extended to all living things, including the smallest insect. When we open our heart, we indeed do feel the sea of suffering in our world. Sometimes we feel good because we can do something to alleviate it. Other times, we feel that we cannot do anything about it, and we feel despondent.

There is a lot of pain in this human life. Sometimes our pain is caused by an outside tragedy, such as the difficult circumstances we go through. Sometimes events shake our world to its core. Other times we feel internal and emotional pain. We are all very vulnerable to that. The sense of being human, of being a person, is also painful because we feel a separation between ourselves and others, a separation between ourselves and the world. As long as this sense of fundamental separation continues in our consciousness, there is always going to be pain, pain that we cannot really describe. It is an existential pain. This pain also causes loneliness that can be deeper than just longing for companionship. The pain of this loneliness won't go away by trying to fill the inner vacuum through acquiring external comforts. It can only be healed through what we might like to call *true transcendence*. This is the goal of many spiritual traditions, even many that don't accept each other's doctrines. True transcendence is the experience that we are no longer trapped in the narrow realm of our ego.

It is often fun to be a human being, but sometimes it is very difficult too. This is true for everybody. Almost every human being has this experience. There is a part of all of us that longs to experience transcendence. Transcendence gives us the feeling that all of our problems are gone. It is the sense that somehow we are one with everything. We don't have to be spiritual to have this longing for transcendence. It is a universal longing. Many people try to experience transcendence by doing things that distract their minds from their problems. This may be the reason many of us love to watch TV, movies, or sporting events. When we go to one of the big sports arenas that often draw thousands and thousands of people, everyone seems to be very happy, even ecstatic. Nobody seems to have a problem. All of their problems are transcended at least for a few hours, and they are swimming in a sea of pure excitement and bliss. Shopping malls, movie theaters, and sports stadiums are places where people can go and experience transcendence. They are like modern versions of churches and temples.

In my tradition one is always cautioned not to be easily impressed by these experiences of transcendence. We use the Tibetan word *nyams* to describe these beautiful, benevolent, transcendent experiences that we can enter, especially during meditation practice. Wise teachers always say, "Do not be impressed by nyams because they are like mist. They will go away very quickly. They are like rainbows." They make us feel that everything is perfect. The problem is that mist and rainbows don't last forever. No matter how beautiful and enchanting they are, at some point they vanish because they are not real. They are like the transcendent experiences we create by going to the mall or attending a big sporting event. These great feelings won't last forever.

One of the few ways that we can realize true transcendence is through practicing the path of compassion. Compassion can help us build our character. We can change ourselves. We don't have to wait for the world to change. That's good news, isn't it? Sometimes we are waiting for the world to change, waiting for it to become more peaceful and more benevolent. Sometimes we are waiting for the people around us to change. We are waiting for them to become kinder toward us so that our life can be perfect. The world doesn't change for us; the world does what it does. People don't change for us either, so we must change ourselves. Somehow, we are beautifully doomed to evolve. The path of compassion is a way to allow us to kindly and nonviolently evolve, to change and keep building our own character. Buddha talked about inner wealth. The notion of inner wealth refers to a spiritual richness in each of us, our human character. Rabia Basri, a famous Sufi mystic from the eighth century, embodied the epitome of such inner wealth. She was assaulted at a very early age. She was physically, emotionally, and sexually abused, but nothing destroyed her inner integrity, and she became a most revered saint.

There is this inner, true wealth in each of us. Each of us has this amazing noble character that cannot be destroyed by suffering or taken away by force. It is the source of true happiness and contentment. The way we develop this inner, noble character is through cultivating the path of compassion. Compassion is an experience that allows us to feel that we are very close to everybody. We lose the feeling that we are separate or different from everybody else. Even though we may not literally feel that we are one with everybody, we realize that we all share some of the same circumstances in life. This helps us lose our tendency to be totally absorbed with ourselves. Much of our suffering comes from being too immersed in our own self-interests. We are constantly thinking about ourselves, trying to protect and defend ourselves. We are very interested in our own well-being, our own security. We fear, sometimes unconsciously, that somebody or something in the outer world, the world of "others," may harm us. This makes us feel lonely and alienated from everybody else. Compassion is the best medicine to cure this illness, the illness of loneliness, isolation, and alienation.

We all long for a special friend, but in the end, compassion is our only special friend. Compassion is a beautiful bridge between ourselves and others. Compassion is defined as the very authentic feeling that we want every living being to be free from suffering and the cause of suffering. We can generate compassion for others, as we do in the Tibetan tradition, by reciting this prayer: "May all living beings be free from suffering and the cause of suffering." In this beautiful practice we visualize other people and invite them into our mind. We literally notice the presence of other people and try to somehow feel what they are feeling. This is beautiful, divine medicine. This is about trying to open our heart and feel firsthand what other people are feeling. We all know what pain is. We all know what sadness is. We all know what fear is. We all know what loneliness is. The sadness and fear that other people are going through is no less painful, no less intense than our own sadness, our own fear, and our own pain. The beautiful practice of compassion opens our heart so that we are not completely lost in the world of "me." We expand our kind awareness, invite everybody into our heart and feel what they are going through.

This method of practicing compassion may sound difficult and even a little bit depressing. Yet it turns out not to be depressing. Somehow, this may be the only spiritual practice that can make us really happy in the end. Compassion is the secret, divine medicine that heals all of our inner suffering. In the end, it fulfills us. Compassion reaches our heart because, in the end, most of our suffering and problems come from being overly focused on ourselves. Compassion takes us away from that mental obsession. Compassion makes us big inside. When we have this all-embracing compassion, we feel that we want to live longer in this world. We want to love humanity more. We experience gratitude constantly and we may also realize that life is an amazing teacher.

The fourth-century Indian master Arya Asanga was a learned monk who went into the forest to meditate for twelve years. When he did not get any results, he experienced great disappointment and left his mountain retreat. Along the way he encountered a sick and injured dog whose wounds were infested with maggots. He felt deep compassion toward the dog, and he wanted to remove the maggots from its wounds. He contemplated how he could remove the maggots from the dog without hurting them. He proceeded to remove them with the tip of his tongue. At this moment he had the profound spiritual experience that he had been looking and praying for without results for the twelve years of his retreat.

If our hearts are open and we can bear witness to the suffering around us, we will be able to act from that and help relieve suffering in whatever small or big ways we can. It will not be insignificant, and our compassion will include all living things, no matter how small they are. Each compassionate act will change us and will expand our boundaries and show us what transcendence means. Then we will begin more and more to lose the feeling that we are separate from everybody else. In this way, we can widen the circle of love.

2

stop, pause, and open
your heart

*M*any teachings are attributed to the Buddha. One collection, known as the *Dhammapada*, is loved by all of the Buddhist traditions. It is a collection of beautiful verses that don't talk about doctrine or about gods and goddesses. Rather it talks about how to live life with love, courage, and wisdom. There is a verse in the *Dhammapada* that says, "With thoughts we create the world." This verse tells us how powerful our thoughts can be. We basically create our sense of reality, our sense of the world, with our own thoughts and our own minds. Happiness and suffering, good and bad, right and wrong are all pretty much creations of our own mind. There can be one hundred people all sitting in a single place at the same time and each person has their own reality. Each one lives entirely in that reality. If we consider one hundred people sharing this moment in time and space, we find that some of them are happy and some of them are extremely depressed. Among these one hundred people, some people experience love and total joy, while others are completely lost in their anger and hatred. Among these one hundred individuals there are people who feel that the universe is extremely beautiful and sacred. They feel gratitude for everything that exists in this world. Others feel that the world is a dangerous, miserable place, full of pain and suffering.

Both of these worldviews are created by the thinking mind. We cannot eliminate our thoughts or our mind. This is not an option; it is impossible. We need our human mind, and we need our thoughts, ideas, and beliefs. We need them to survive as a human species. Our entire system, our psyche, even our biology is designed to survive only through the thinking mind. Our human mind sees everything as being made out of similar patterns, and we label those patterns. We divide and categorize them into this and that. That gives us a sense of being an individual and having our own life. We believe that we are avoiding danger and following our passion. Yet when we totally believe those thoughts and patterns, we can be completely lost in our mind and out of touch with reality. Then there is a high price to pay for our misconceptions. As human beings we have been paying this high price for a very long time without really waking up.

Buddhist teachings say that all of our problems come from unawareness, from not being aware of how things really are. In that sense, meditation is about creating a pause in our consciousness. We can step away from our mind and recognize our personal thoughts and beliefs. We can challenge them so we don't end up being completely caught up in them. Believing our mind and every thought that arises in our head is actually the root of all of our problems. The truth is that a huge portion of the world's population is living every day in this unawareness, completely lost in their mind and in their thoughts. It's no wonder that there are so many problems in the world as well as in our personal lives. The root of suffering is actually quite easy to figure out. There is no mystery. It does not take sophisticated philosophical analysis to figure out our human suffering. It comes from believing our mind and not challenging our ideas and assumptions. A powerful spiritual practice is to pause and stop believing our mind for a while. If we can remember to do this, it can actually change us. It can transform our consciousness.

Many of us are very good at learning new Buddhist methodologies and techniques. Outwardly we are very devoted to practice. But we are not good at one practice that is extremely important, a practice that can produce the transformation that many of us are seeking. Many of us do not practice the discipline of pausing to stop believing in our own mind. Most often we accept our mind's thoughts as true. We accept what it comes up with without any questions. When we believe our mind, we often judge others and feel anger toward them. We can even feel hatred for them. This causes us to feel separate from others. Not only do we feel separate from them, we feel that they are different, and we lose our sense of the interconnection that we share. We lose touch with life's great mystery. Our hearts can become closed, and we are not able to experience all-pervasive sacredness, the sacredness of everything that exists, the sacredness of each and every being in this universe. We can adopt the practice of questioning the beliefs and positions our mind comes up with. We can stop and pause and question if these thoughts are actually true in reality or if they are based on old assumptions and old patterns of behavior.

Even though this is the twenty-first century and our world is very advanced in many ways, we are still collectively very unaware. All of the problems we face are due to this unawareness. We are always dealing with it. We are suffering now because there is more collective unawareness than there is collective awareness. We would all like to see this change. We would like to see the force of awareness become stronger than the force of unawareness. Some of us may think that the solution to the problem is to have more meditators or more Buddhists. Maybe if we could achieve that, then everything would be fine. But that is not the solution. There are many meditators out there; we do not have a shortage of meditators. But we are not changing the world because, unfortunately, we are repeating the same vicious cycle of believing our thoughts, believing our mind.

Buddha taught awareness. His very name means "the awakened one," the one who is aware. What does it mean to be aware? In one important sense it means to be aware of our mind and to stop believing thoughts that arise from projections and psychological patterns. Awareness is a state of consciousness in which we are no longer investing in thoughts that arise from projections and patterns. Unawareness, on the other hand, is a state of being lost in these thoughts, mental projections, and confabulations. Such unaware thoughts might arise from anxiety, fear, or resentment. Awareness happens when we challenge these thoughts. Right now, unawareness is the stronger force in the world.

Fortunately, awareness is also a powerful force. There are times when people come together and create what I call a "sacred container." We have a sacred container when people create an intention, either individually or collectively, to wake up and open their hearts. They work to step away from their mind, away from their thoughts, their beliefs, and their habitual emotional tendencies. Within this sacred container is the force of awareness. The whole world is, indeed, not a sacred container. It's a world of unawareness most of the time. We have to accept that and still we have to open our hearts and love this world along with its unawareness, pain, and violence. This is not about rejecting the world and creating some kind of sacred container secluded somewhere in a beautiful forest or high in the mountains. That does not work. When unawareness is the more predominating force, then unawareness feeds on itself. My unawareness can actually feed somebody else's unawareness, and that person's unawareness can feed someone else's unawareness. That's how unawareness works.

Unawareness can also be juicy. It comes with aggression, violence, hatred, and all kinds of concepts. Remember that during the time of the Roman Empire many coliseums were built and within these coliseums horrible crimes were committed. These crimes were turned into fantastic entertainment. People were totally insensitive. They cheered and were amused. That was the ultimate entertainment in the times of the Roman Empire. It is hard to imagine that people killing other people was considered entertainment. It's hard to imagine that seeing gladiators and wild animals killing each other without any sadness, without any sensitivity, was amusing and entertaining. It's hard to imagine that it was accompanied by shouting and laughing.

So, the question is, as mature, responsible human beings, what do we want to do with this world? What influence can we have on these messy situations of unawareness, anger, even hatred in our relationships with each other, with other living entities, and with our planet? How can we change the situation? There is only one answer. We must keep opening our hearts. It is true that there is a lot of violence, separation, hatred, and fear. But we can remember that every human being is our cousin, our niece, or our nephew. The point is to not close our hearts no matter how difficult it sometimes becomes. Even when things are disappointing and harsh, we can still open our hearts to humanity, to suffering, and to the world. There is no us versus them. There is only one large, diverse family. We cannot reject anybody. We can't reject any group of people. All of humanity is one huge family. Sometimes it is a wonderful family, and other times it is a dysfunctional family, but because we are one family, we cannot throw anybody out of the house. We realize that every human being is our brother or sister. Every human being is our cousin, our niece, or our nephew. The point is to not close our hearts no matter how difficult it is with situations in our own life as well as with situations in the world.

Let's love this world again. Let's love this world even though there is collective unawareness. Let's open our hearts to the world, to humanity, and to suffering. When we see things from the other's point of view, we can see and feel their suffering. Then it is much easier to forgive. We have more room to think and act on our own. We have more choices. Each of us can be a beacon, a lamp, a light of awareness, and we can offer an amazing gift to this beloved human world and to our beloved human brothers and sisters.

3

one family

One of the strongest impulses we all have is our desire to experience transcendence. When we tap into transcendence we rise above all of our concerns. We are no longer dominated by fear and we are no longer caught up in the web of worldly affairs, which come with anxiety and worry. That's why transcendence is desirable. Now and then we have moments when we literally rise above all of our personal issues and the worldly affairs that concern us. We have a larger, more expanded view. Everything is fine because we become one with a bigger reality. We call this transcendence. At the same time, we cannot deny what is happening in the world: war, violence, and a great deal of suffering from many causes. Even though we have amazing moments when we rise above everything and transcend reality, in the end we always have to come back to whatever is happening in our personal lives as well as in the world at large.

Many of us feel transcendence during meditation or prayer. It's wonderful and inspiring to experience. It's a break that we all need. Yet we cannot live forever in that realm. We have to come back. We cannot deny reality even though it can sometimes be very unpleasant. We might try to understand it and why it is happening. One of the best ways to understand reality is to look at the theory of karma. The theory of karma is very important wisdom cherished by both Hindus and Buddhists. It's not really a theory or a doctrine. Rather it is a living wisdom that applies to issues on personal, societal, and world levels. That wisdom can help us understand the very complex and dynamic nature of all conditions.

The concept of karma is not new. The word or concept of karma can be found everywhere, even in songs and pop music. When something bad happens, people often say, "It's my karma." Sometimes they say, "It's your karma." Of course, if we say that to someone, they might be offended because it sounds like we are saying it is their fault. However, in Tibetan culture when you say, "It's my (or your) karma," there is a sense of surrender, acceptance, peace, compassion, and wisdom. When we see someone who is going through a difficult situation, and we say with love and a kind heart that it's their karma, they understand. They don't feel that we are being coldhearted or insensitive. They take it as spiritual advice, as a wonderful reminder, a reminder of the wisdom teachings of the awakened ones.

Buddhist and Hindu traditions have a deep understanding of karma, and they use its theories to understand the complex, dynamic nature of life. One answer for what is happening in the world right now is because it's our karma. To say it is our karma means that it is happening because of a complex interconnection of causes and conditions. In Buddhist thinking everything comes into being through causes and conditions. Nothing is purely random or accidental. Everything we are witnessing right now, both at a personal level and at the larger societal level, is the consequence of a myriad of causes and conditions. It is the fruition of all of the choices that people have made over time along with the choices people are making today. It includes the choices that you and I make today as well as the choices our parents, grandparents, and ancestors made. It also includes the actions that they took and the state of consciousness in which they lived.

Karma teaches us that every action that we take has a very powerful impact. It also reminds us that the state of consciousness in which we live has a long-term impact on our own life as well as on the lives of the people around us. Look at nature. Nature is perhaps one of the most powerful teachers. Today we are witnessing a host of ecological crises, including earthquakes, fires, and climate change. Much of this environmental crisis is a result of human action. From that perspective we can see that the actions we take or do not take have a great impact, an impact that goes beyond our own personal life. The ecological crisis is a human creation, even though some people deny it. As humanity, we all created it together. Its reality is a karmic manifestation that we can no longer deny. We are all witnessing this law of karma.

Buddhism teaches that just as our actions have karmic results, the state of our consciousness has karmic results as well. That's why it is very important to look inside and make sure that we are choosing the state of consciousness we want to live in. We can choose to reside in an unenlightened state of consciousness, or we can choose to reside in a more enlightened state. In the more enlightened state there is more love, more compassion, and more of a sense that we are all in this together. While the theory of karma teaches us that the environmental conditions happening now are somehow a result of our own actions, it also teaches that we can do something about them. There is no fate that we cannot change. We can take actions to change the course of the future. We have the power to reshape the future—our own future as well as the future of humanity. It teaches us that all of the circumstances and conditions we experience in life are a manifestation of the state of mind that we choose to reside in. This is true because the state of our mind determines the actions we take. From the point of view of collective karma, everything that is happening in the world is no longer someone else's karma. It's our karma. In the end your karma is my karma, and my karma is your karma. We all share the same fate.

The twelfth-century Indian sage Padampa Sangye, in his teaching called *Advice to the People of Tingri*, advised us to hold the view that the whole world is our land, our community, and our tribe. He said you cannot exclude anybody from your heart. You have to widen your heart and embrace the whole world as your neighborhood and all living beings as your brothers and sisters. You have to be willing to share their pain and suffering as well as their happiness and joy. Collective karma teaches that it is not wise to try and divide humanity. It teaches us to transcend all divisions. We often create a division by thinking that our group or tribe is the wise, enlightened, and evolved tribe, the ones who always make the right decisions, while other groups are the more primitive, unenlightened, and unevolved ones who make bad decisions. It is easy to make these unhealthy divisions, but Padampa tells us that any kind of division is unhealthy and merely the work of the ego. He urges us to widen our heart and embrace all of humanity because there are no divisions. There is only one world and only one race. We are all family members. Imagine that a member of your family, someone that you love completely and unconditionally, was going through some difficulty. You naturally want to help them. You want to share both the happiness and the suffering of your family members. It would be very powerful if we could imagine that all of humanity is our family. Actually, we are just one big family. Our family members may say things, do things, and demonstrate a state of consciousness that completely challenges us. But they are family, and in the end, the wise response is to have compassion.

Recently there was a story in the news about two young boys who were swimming in the ocean and got into trouble in a riptide that was very strong. They were unable to swim back to shore. Some of their family members swam out to help them, but they too got caught in the riptide. Soon there were nine people stranded in the ocean unable to reach shore. People on the beach noticed what was happening, and they stepped in. They made a human chain by holding hands. The line extended from the beach into the water where the people were stranded. One by one those family members grabbed onto the hands of the human chain and were able to make it back to shore. All of the swimmers were saved. No one was injured. This true story proves the power we have when we can act together to care for strangers in need. We can help each other a great deal.

We need to have compassion for ourselves and for all of humanity because we are all carrying this very heavy burden of karma. This heavy burden of pain and suffering. No one escapes this. So, we have to have acceptance and forgiveness for ourselves and all of humanity. Basically, we need to give everybody a little bit of time: time to grow, time to make mistakes, and time to become more mature. We are all here on earth for a very short period of time. We have to have compassion and understanding for all. We have to accept who we are, accept our suffering, our mistakes, the wrong choices we make, and the state of consciousness that we as a whole society live in.

The theory of karma is very empowering. It teaches us that we can change our ourselves and we can change our situation. Sometimes change doesn't happen overnight, but we can at least take actions that begin to change our collective karma. Buddhism teaches that karma is not just the action that we take but also the state of consciousness that we choose to reside in. Mental karma is one of the most powerful forces in the world because every action we take comes from our mental states, what we believe to be true. Our mind is the very thing that determines the nature and quality of the words we utter and every action we take. The best way to change the world is through developing love for ourselves, for each other, and for all living things that share our beautiful earth. Love is a very powerful force. In Tibetan culture, there is a saying. "When there is a good heart, everything is going to be okay." The good heart is the true nature of all of us. Let's hold that good heart for everyone—for ourselves, our world, and all of humanity.

4

the one you feed

In Buddhist traditions there is a state of mind that is called the *mind of disenchantment*. The mind of disenchantment comes about when we look inside and witness the deep-seated thoughts and emotional patterns of our mind. Our mind has tendencies, habitual patterns of anger, fear, greed, hatred, and jealousy. When we look inside, we often see that our behavior is unconsciously ruled by these negative tendencies and habitual patterns of our mind. We come to the feeling that we are almost terrified by the power of the unawakened state of our own consciousness, which is called *samsara*. It is very useful to do this kind of reflection. It would be really nice if more people in the world did it too.

Cultivating a mind of disenchantment does not sound interesting or enticing. However, I recommend that we all try this reflection now and then. Other spiritual practices like learning how to be happy and joyous sound much more productive. This one sounds almost counterproductive. Yet it is an essential reflection for anyone who wants to change themself. I strongly recommend that we each take this reflection and practice it in our everyday life.

Look at your mind thoroughly and honestly and see all of its tendencies. You'll see there is fear, anger, judgment, guilt, and shame. There is so much of this in our mind, yet usually we don't recognize it. When we do, we can be literally terrified of our own mind. But this is good news, not bad news. Perhaps we all should be terrified by our own mind from time to time. When we are terrified by our mind, it does not mean that we are more deluded or more messed up than other people. Just the opposite. It is an indication that we are more awake and more mindful. It is an indication that we are evolving. This reflection will bring about a whole new level of awakening and transformation in our hearts and minds.

When I was young, I spent a lot of time with my teacher Lama Tsurlo. I was very young when I met him, and I didn't know very much about Buddhist practices or about the reflections and contemplations they teach. I always wanted to spend time with Lama Tsurlo, but at the same time I was very afraid of him. I didn't have any idea of the reason behind my fear. My fear was totally irrational. Lama Tsurlo was a very gentle man; he was also disabled. He walked with a limp. Although he was extremely kind, I was afraid of sitting in his presence. At the same time, I wanted to spend a lot of time with him and I didn't know where the fear was coming from. If he had been abusive to me, then it would have made sense for me to be afraid of sitting in his presence, but he was very, very kind. I used to feel that he could read my mind because he was so awake. There was a part of me that didn't want him to read my mind. It's like not wanting to invite a special guest over when your house is messy and filled with junk. It's like waking up and remembering that somebody is coming to visit you, but somehow you slept late and forgot to vacuum and clean the table. The point is that in those years I didn't have the courage to really look at my own mind and feel either what they call the fear of samsara or the mind of disenchantment. But somehow, I felt intuitively that my master was reading my mind all of the time. Perhaps he was reading my mind not as a result of clairvoyance but just because he was very mature and wise. Sometimes you can figure out kind of intuitively what is happening in other people's minds.

I ask you—in fact, I really beg you—to practice this radical reflection. Please make sure that you are extremely frightened by your own mind. Not all of the time, but now and then. It would be nice if many people in the world, from all walks of life, decided to do this radical reflection. Once you experience this extraordinary, benevolent fear of your mind, you will have the desire and motivation to change yourself and change your consciousness.

There is a beautiful story, often attributed to Native Americans, about a grandfather and his grandson. The grandfather said, "There is a war going on inside of me. It is a very ugly fight."

His grandson asked, "What kind of war is it?"

The grandfather replied, "It is a fight between two wolves. One is this evil wolf that is malicious, hateful, angry, stingy, passive-aggressive, self-pitying, and arrogant, with both superiority and inferiority complexes. The other wolf is very benevolent, carefree, joyous, forgiving, humorous, compassionate, courageous, loving, generous, and openhearted."

His grandson asked, "Who will win this war?"

The grandfather answered, "The one you feed the most."

This is an inspiring story that we should all remember and share with others. The extraordinarily wise grandfather was able to be

23

aware of this war going on inside. For many people, there isn't even a war because they have not yet become aware of it. It takes introspection and self-reflection to become aware of this war. Indeed, for many people the wolf of fear and greed is always winning, and for many people he wins pretty much every day. Many people identify with the wolf that embodies all the negativities. The war the grandfather was aware of is an experience that many people become aware of on the spiritual journey. This inner war is depicted in the sacred epics and stories of many spiritual traditions.

Once we turn our attention inward, we can see the war between these two wolves, and then we have a choice about which one we want to feed. We can feed the wolf of fear, judgment, anger, self-pity, and passive-aggressiveness, or we can feed the wolf of love, kindness, compassion, generosity, and so forth. Theoretically we might think that most people, once they become aware of the internal war, would naturally choose to feed the good wolf. But that is not the case. Sometimes we intentionally feed this dangerous wolf. Sometimes it's for psychological reasons. We do it as a resistance strategy or as an internal defense because we don't want to face something that may be very painful.

The writer James Baldwin once said, "I imagine one of the reasons people cling to their hate so stubbornly is because once the hate is gone, they will be forced to deal with the pain." This is a powerful statement that we all have to reckon with. Baldwin points out that we can use hatred to deflect our attention away from a wounded heart and the sense of being traumatized or defeated. Or we may feel guilt and shame. Many people don't want to experience these negative feelings, so they resort to hatred. That is not something that just a few people do. This is something that a whole culture sometimes does. There is collective hatred in every culture, and sometimes people intentionally hold on to this hatred because it makes them feel that they are right, strong, and powerful. As the wise grandfather said, this war is happening all of the time in each of us. We might want to look inside to see the layers of resistance and the unconscious strategies we have that continuously feed this dangerous wolf because we don't want to experience pain. The truth is, we always have a choice.

It's good to feel the fear of being terrified by our own mind. Buddha experienced this fear. In his teachings he said that he was terrified by the violence and insanity that exists in the world. Of course, we don't have to live in this fear all of the time. However, it is important to find time here and there, perhaps a few times a week, to sit and to literally feel this divine fear. The point is to always be mindful if we can. To be mindful means that in one way or another we are observing our mind. We observe what is happening inside and see the thoughts, feelings, and emotions we are experiencing in that very moment, without judgment but at the same time creating a space where we are not indulging in them. We then have the choice not to feed the dangerous wolf. Sometimes when we look, we see that the dangerous wolf is very active and powerful. He is actually winning. Then, in that very moment, we have the choice not to feed it. That's all we have to do, not feed it.

Other times we might like to look inside and feed the benevolent wolf. There are many ways of feeding that benevolent wolf. We can practice what Tibetans call "a good heart." The Tibetan masters developed amazing, very practical techniques for feeding the benevolent wolf by cultivating loving-kindness and compassion. They cultivated enlightened mind with techniques such as this. When opening a door, tell your mind, "I am opening the door to the city of liberation for every living being." When washing the dishes or your hands, say, "I am washing the sorrow off all living beings." When you are walking, tell your mind, "I am leading all human beings to the city of liberation, the city of nirvana." It's not really logical, but can you see that by cultivating these amazing, radical thoughts, you can change your mind. You can intentionally feed that benevolent wolf. If we could capture the essence of a good heart in one simple phrase, it would be, "May I benefit all living beings." When we take a few seconds to recite this phrase, we can see that our heart opens and our consciousness expands. We can see the difference between these wonderful, benevolent thoughts and thoughts that have to do with judgment and hatred. Benevolent thoughts have great power on our consciousness.

Reciting verses in the morning can be very productive. The verses help us set up the right intention for our day. This is very powerful. But we don't have to use traditional verses; we can compose our own sacred verses to recite. We can say something like, "Today I am going to be mindful. I'm going to live with awareness. I'm going to feed that benevolent wolf, and I am not going to feed that dangerous wolf." If we remember to recite this verse every day, perhaps we'll notice that our consciousness is changing. We could also say, "May I benefit all living beings here and there." When we say these verses, either out loud or in silence, they actually become a mantra. *Mantra* can be defined as that which liberates the mind. *Man* is "mind," and *tra* is "to protect." That is one way to define the word mantra. Mantra can be regarded as an incantation to protect our mind from the bad wolf. We can recite our mantra or benevolent phrase either out loud or silently to transform our mind and our heart. Once we start to incorporate this mantra into our life, we will soon see a positive result in the form of the inner change of our heart and mind.

5

widen the circle of love
and compassion

We all have consciousness. When we open our eyes, we may see form, color, and movement. Our ears may hear voices and sounds. It is our consciousness that is aware of all of this content. Consciousness can be very extraordinary; we can experience love and compassion. But sometimes we can be a little bit lost, especially when our consciousness becomes aware of itself and develops the sense of a separate self. This is the experience that there is "me" and then there is the world "out there." Then we develop the sense that I am separate from everybody and everything else. In Buddhist teachings, this experience is often described as the *primordial delusion*.

When we experience that we are separate from everything else, we determine that there are things that are good for us. We naturally develop an attraction, a desire, and a grasping toward whatever we perceive those good things to be. These things give us comfort and security. Then we also determine that there are things that are not so good for us. These are things that usually present a challenge or a threat to us. We naturally develop an aversion, perhaps anger or feelings of being challenged or even repulsed by them. Sometimes we act out of those experiences of aversion and anger, and these acts can cause harm and inflict pain on others.

The experiences of liking and not liking, of grasping and aversion, are very strong in our psyche. They don't go away easily. They stay in our psyche for a long time and they influence and color our perception of reality and therefore many of the important decisions we make. Experiences of liking are so strong that Buddha called them cravings. He put these cravings into three categories: craving for pleasure, craving for existence, and craving for nonexistence. These cravings are tendencies that are so deeply rooted in our system that we might not be able to change them right away. The concept of three cravings is important for understanding the primary root of human misery. Because Buddha discovered that all of our misery—anxiety, worry, fear, or hatred—originally came from one of those three cravings.

We can associate the craving for existence with our desire and grasping toward the things that our mind perceives are good for us. Among the things we desire are things or objects that we want to acquire or keep from losing. We can also get overly attached to a person or a relationship. We get attached to many things. For example, we get attached to material objects. Big things like houses and cars as well as little things like shoes, toothbrushes, and cell phones. Our ego perceives that these things make us happier and more comfortable. They give us comfort, security, and existence to some degree. We also get attached to people and relationships. When we are overly attached, we tend to take refuge in people we like or love and also in our relationships. Recently a friend of mine told me she was falling apart because her relationship of twenty-five years came to a sudden and unexpected end. I reminded her that someday down the road, maybe in ten years or even sooner, this whole experience that was so upsetting now would be just a memory. "Someday you will be laughing and dancing while you are telling people that ten years ago you were falling apart."

Sometimes we get very attached to people, relationships, and material things not because they are great, not because they are amazing, but because our ego identifies with them. Our ego feels that these things bring us security, comfort, and certainty. Then we can get lost in an unhealthy attachment, a fixation, or even an obsession. We can develop a fixation not just to people but to almost anything. Often our fixation, our unhealthy attachment, is not logical or rational. However, we don't recognize that. Usually when we are attached to something, when we are obsessed with something, we feel with our whole being that our attachment is very reasonable, very logical.

Imagine that someone was attached to their smartphone. They believe that their smartphone is the most amazing object in the universe. They believe that they just can't get along without it. Without it, life would be empty. Or imagine that someone is attached to a person they are in a relationship with. They may feel that this person descended from heaven just for them. They came just to comfort and adore them. They come to believe that they can't live without him or her. When we believe this wholeheartedly, we get lost in that experience. Our rational logic is gone because we are completely ruled by our deep-seated tendencies and patterns. We simply don't know that our experiences are not logical. It all has to

31

do with our ego, which perceives that it is separate from everyone and everything in the world.

On the other hand, ego perceives that there are things that are dangerous and harmful to us. They challenge us and make us feel bad. These things, people, and situations then somehow invoke our aversion, our anger, our hatred. We may perceive that some people are dangerous to us or they are not lovable. They may make us feel unhappy or repulsed. When we don't know that these perceptions are irrational, we can get lost in them, and what comes out of them is violence. I'm not saying that there are not some situations that are dangerous and harmful, situations that we should be alert about and should avoid. But sometimes we overreact and create illogical reasons for not caring for someone or some group of people. These situations have to do with covering up and hiding from our own pain, a pain that has little to do with them.

Recently a friend of mine shared an amazing insight. She said that she loved volunteering in our spiritual community. She said, "I am happy, I'm inspired, I'm excited. I feel like I am doing something meaningful, and I always want to talk with the wonderful people in this community. They are so friendly and interesting. But I noticed that I don't want to talk with my mother most of the time, and I don't want to spend time with her." She said she wished she had the same desire to talk to her mom. She wished she wanted to spend time with her mom as much as she wanted to spend time in the spiritual community. This is actually a profound awakening.

In Tibetan culture, loving our parents and making peace with them is the most important duty in life. There is this notion that we must know how to make peace with them; otherwise we will never know how to make peace with ourselves or anybody else. Tibetans tend to feel this moral contentment once they feel that they have built a peaceful relationship with their parents before they go away from this world. Our parents are the first people that we can work with to practice acceptance, forgiveness, and unconditional love. We can learn to love them and find joy in helping them. Anyway, what this person said was extremely insightful, as well as deeply moving and profound. Basically, she said, "I have a preference." That's the word she used—*preference*. We all have preferences, but most of the time we don't notice them. Let's call them the "demons of preference." We all have demons of preference, and when we look deeply inside, we recognize them. Then we can choose if they are reasonable or not, if they are helpful or harmful to ourselves as well as other people. Without this insightful examination, this demon of preference can completely dominate our consciousness and limit our capacity to love, to exercise compassion, and to feel our connection and interdependence with every other human being.

One of my all-time favorite quotes is by Albert Einstein. He wrote, "A human being is a part of the whole called by us universe, a part limited in time and space. He experiences himself, his thoughts and feelings as something separated from the rest, a kind of optical delusion of his consciousness. This delusion is like a prison for us, restricting us to our personal desires and to affection for a few persons nearest to us. Our task must be to free ourselves from this prison by widening our circle of compassion to embrace all living creatures and the whole of nature in its beauty."

Einstein said that the purpose of our human life is to widen the circle of love and compassion to include all living creatures and the whole of nature in its beauty. Now we can relax about trying to figure out what the purpose of life is. Einstein has figured it out and already said what it is. It is to widen the circle of love and compassion toward all living beings. Usually we have to question what people say. But in this case, I believe that we can trust Albert Einstein.

If we are ruled by this demon of preference, it becomes a very powerful hindrance that holds us back from developing a heart-felt connection with other human beings and, in the end, with all humanity, with all living things. It also holds us back from acquiring self-knowledge. The most ancient adepts said that if we really want to be free, if we really want to evolve and wake up, the secret lies in acquiring self-knowledge. Buddha also taught this. Here *self-knowledge* means being aware of our limitations and negative tendencies. It means knowing our shadow, knowing our greed, knowing our neuroses. We might like to look inside and recognize that we all have this demon of preference. Recognizing it is very powerful and enlightening. Not recognizing it holds us back from awakening, from evolving, and from expanding the circle of love and compassion.

When we look, we may see that this demon often operates in our psyche unconsciously. For example, when we go to parties or other gatherings, we might notice that we like to talk to some people more than others. Some people seem so much more attractive, likable, and interesting than others. We may also notice that we are avoiding, consciously or unconsciously, certain other people. Perhaps they seem unattractive and uninteresting for some often-unknown reason. But they are not intrinsically uninteresting. When we experience others as uninteresting and unattractive, what we are usually experiencing is simply a part of ourselves. We are projecting that part of ourselves onto someone else. When we go to parties or even walk down the street, we notice that sometimes, maybe even unconsciously, we are avoiding some people because of the demon of preference.

Recently I heard about a very interesting program about the topic of "implicit bias." I had never heard the term before, but when the program's organizer explained it, I recognized it as one of the characteristics we all have. She said unconsciously or in the subconscious we all have deep-seated tendencies to judge other people based on their color, race, gender, and social status. These biases do not have any intrinsic truth. They are actually an expression of delusion, primordial ignorance. They do not rest in the truth. They are simply an expression of delusion. It's called *dualism*. The extraordinary ancient mystics like Machig Labdrön, the renowned eleventh-century yogini, intentionally spent a lot of time with beggars and people with leprosy. Her spiritual practice was to recognize the inner demon of preference and to overcome it. She went out and visited and spent time with people who are less fortunate, such as beggars. She even hung out with lepers who had been ostracized from the human community. Doing such things during those days was an incredible act of selflessness.

My invitation to all of us is to go inside and be courageous. Don't be afraid of embracing this demon of preference. Let's acknowledge that we have it and recognize it for what it is: a powerful hindrance. All we have to do is be aware of it. Once we become aware of it, we can walk the path of the heart. Maybe our spiritual practice is to talk with someone we don't necessarily want to talk with, or to spend time with someone we feel we have a difference with. Maybe we can send a kind letter to somebody we have differences with. We can walk the path of *bodhicitta*, the awakened heart. Then we are truly widening the circle of love and compassion to include all living creatures and the whole of nature in its beauty. We are then, as Albert Einstein said, fulfilling the true purpose of our life.

6

be the lamp

*M*any traditions teach that there is an original purity in all of us. This original purity, our own fundamental goodness, is also our true nature. It is not a physical dimension; it is a profound realm that lies within. From it we can channel love, compassion, courage, and wisdom. Every human being has this infinite source within, yet it is also true that many in our world are not living examples of love and compassion. There is a lot of hatred and aggression in our world, and unfortunately, we find that in almost every culture.

Buddhist traditions use the term *klesha,* which literally means "internal affliction," to name these powerful forces that often veil our true nature. These forces, this energy, can be psychological or even karmic phenomena. Not only do these negative forces veil our true nature, they also become powerful hindrances that prevent us from evolving, from transforming. They encompass our neurotic tendencies. While they are not intrinsically bad in themselves, they can completely obscure our true nature, our original purity, especially when we are not aware of them. These hindrances are dormant most of the time, but an unsettling event, a challenge, often triggers or activates them. The unsettling event or challenge can trigger these forces, such as fear, anxiety, or hatred. Whatever it is, those powerful hindrances or negative emotions already exist in each of us. We usually think that somebody else is making us anxious, angry, or fearful. But the anger, fear, and anxiety are already in each of us, and the circumstances merely triggered them and brought them to the surface.

Life is always dancing. It does what it does. It is outside of our control, and we have very little power to influence the grand scheme of things. Sometimes life dances in a way that delights us, and sometimes it dances in a way that challenges our desires, our preferences, and our aspirations. But we should always remember that these neurotic tendencies are already there. Ultimately nobody is making us fearful. It's just external events that sometimes challenge us and trigger our own tendencies and habitual patterns.

We go through periods of life where events don't agree with our preferences. This happens more often than we want. It happens in our personal life and it happens in larger contexts, like world events and political affairs. Remembering this alone is going to bring so much peace to our heart. This idea is simple but might be hard to bring into everyday life and to apply in the face of any kind of challenge. It might not be natural to our brain, which goes immediately into the mode of fight-or-flight response. Our human brain is similar to that of animals. It's always seeking out potential threats that can endanger us. This neurological function can be useful as survival intelligence. As a fragile species in the face of an unfriendly world, we humans might never have survived without it. The problem is that when fight-or-flight takes over, we react out of proportion to the way things are. It takes time and effort to rewire our brain's behavior. We have to be diligent and consistent in order to change our mental habits. It's like trying to keep your teeth healthy. It's not enough to brush them just once in a while.

Much of the time we don't closely follow politics, social issues, or world affairs. We are usually extremely preoccupied with our own personal lives. Most challenges that trigger our neurotic tendencies have something to do with our health, our financial situation, or the loss of our loved ones. However, periodically there are external events, world events that influence us, and then we become either very excited or challenged to our core by these circumstances. We are at a very interesting time in human history. We can no longer create a little bubble to live in. We can't shut down our awareness of the larger events that are happening in the world. We can no longer be an island, simply concerned with our own self-interests. Our world has grown smaller, and we are all connected with everybody else in this world. Countries, nations, and tribes are interconnected with each other more than ever. Our futures are linked.

Sometimes we have good ideas and hopes for our own people and our own country. We could be living under an innocent illusion or even an expectation about our own people, our own country. Then something happens, an event occurs, and we may be shocked to realize that our country is not the country we thought it was. It may not be as altruistic and honorable as we thought it was. It may not be headed in the direction we believe is the best for our future or for the future of the world. We realize there may be devolution rather than evolution. This is a moment to go inside and try to be the source of change instead of hoping that the world will change in accordance with our own high ideals and principles.

One thing we can do is not fall into the old trap of *reacting*. Usually when there is challenge, we tend to react. Reaction is mechanical. It does not come from equanimity or compassion. It does not include an understanding of the human condition. Reaction usually includes judgment, anger, and even hatred. Reaction can be a source of disharmony that adds to divisiveness in the human family. It can turn into aggression and eventually escalate into strife, violence, and war. When change is needed, it means that this is a time for all of us to be the change. We can be the lamp that illuminates the consciousness that may someday illuminate the world.

As long as humanity continues this old habit of reacting, negativities perpetuate. Unawareness feeds them, and they don't go away on their own. Though they are psychic entities and have no form or shape, they are powerful forces. For example, when we feel angry, fearful, or anxious, these feelings exert an almost physical force over us. They can completely seize and run away with us. They tend to sustain or perpetuate their existence in each of us as long as we are unaware of them and their power. Our unawareness feeds these negative feelings. But if nothing feeds them, eventually they dissolve. This is why all the ancient masters said that the root of human struggle in this human world is actually *avidya*, or unawareness.

Some unpleasant events are happening in our world right now. They are causing much division, aggression, and hatred. These are not signs that some human beings are intrinsically flawed, that they are not good. It does not mean there are divisions among human beings, that there are good people versus bad people. It does not mean that "we" are the enlightened ones and "they" are the not-so-enlightened ones, that "we" are the evolved ones and "they" are not so evolved. All of these events, all of these incidents are just reflections that there is too much unawareness in this world. It is everywhere, not just in this country. It is everywhere. We have to open our hearts and embrace everyone, even people who hold a view that is totally opposed to ours. We have to know that we are all subject to this unawareness. Unawareness exists in each of us, but it manifests in different ways.

Fear is very strong right now. When there is fear, there is hatred. This is very toxic. The first thing we should do as human beings is to go inside and recognize our own negative habitual patterns. We should recognize what triggers these. Without that recognition, there won't be any authentic change in us. The world cannot change unless we start changing in an authentic way. Once we have that recognition, that self-knowledge, we have a choice. We can respond differently to situations that challenge us. Life constantly challenges us. It provides endless catalysts to trigger our neurotic tendencies. Even the smallest event can completely throw us off balance.

Our tendency to be triggered by small events is why there is road rage. You might have read headlines in the newspaper mentioning road rage. Person A cut off person B, and person B became so furious that he or she shot person A. This seems totally beyond our comprehension, but it happens. It is rather unbelievable that a small event, an almost insignificant event, can trigger so much rage that we lose our compassion, our reverence for life. It seems absurd that we can go so far as to hurt another human being without considering the consequences to that person and their family members. This is a powerful example of how something simple can set off a chain reaction that leads to a huge tragedy. This happens with small events in our personal lives, as well as in large events that play out globally. The process is the same. But in fact, we are not so different from the person who acted out of road rage. That person is one of us. We can fall into unawareness in many ways, and before we know it, we are reacting with judgment and anger. We may not react by picking up weapons, but we react in ways that are often violent and destructive.

Many wise men and women talk about the "center of our being." This is a place in each of us where we can go and ground ourselves. The center of our being is like the eye of a storm. No matter how much chaos or craziness is happening around us, or even inside us, this place is a true sanctuary, a true refuge. It is a place where we can be in touch with the best part of ourselves; a place where we are not shaken, not challenged, not pushed back and forth by either internal or external chaos. The center of our being is a place where we can feel and act from our own compassion and courage. Many practices in the Buddhist tradition, including meditation, are designed as tools that allow us to find that place. Once we know how to find that place, we can experience an amazing stillness. From here we have the ability to choose to act rather than react. And the less we react, the more our negative tendencies become insignificant in our consciousness. Eventually we experience an amazing transformation. In Buddhism we say, "Wearing out." It means these tendencies wear out. When we have a commitment to walk the path of awareness, we will see this amazing transformation. Our fear, hatred, shame, guilt, and all tendencies of reacting begin to subside. They wear out. This is what inner transformation looks like.

It doesn't happen overnight, and it doesn't happen in some kind of beautiful, magical way. It happens gradually, and it happens because we choose to act rather than react in habitual, negative ways. We choose through awareness to hold others in compassion.

Perhaps our best contribution to our world is actually to go inside and practice awareness. Then we can find the center of our being and remember that there is original purity in us and in everyone else. We are all intrinsically good human beings. When we act from this place, our actions can be a true contribution to all of the challenges we face. We can act in ways that are personally fulfilling and we can act in ways that help our world, ways that lessen the suffering of all. We can begin to build the kind of world we want to see, the kind of world our children and all the world's children can live in. It is a goal worth working toward.

7

walking in beauty

*P*erhaps many of the problems that we face each day, both globally and personally, come from disconnecting with the sacred. The experience of the sacred is something essential that we are missing right now in this world. We can awaken to this experience by opening our hearts. When we open our hearts, the sacred is something we can all taste and feel. The experience of the sacred is not an idea or concept. It is not simply an esoteric belief. Of course, it can be turned into a concept or belief. When that happens, we are cut off from something very precious and vital. This can lead to a host of problems. We can forget that nature, the environment that surrounds and nurtures us, is rare and precious. We can forget that it is sacred and forget that we ourselves are sacred too. Every human being is sacred. Can you imagine how amazing it would be if humanity suddenly woke up and realized and treated each other accordingly? We would live in a very different world, a much more loving, peaceful, and joyful world.

The result of not remembering that every human being is sacred is that we develop jealousy, judgment, competition, and aggression toward each other. Violence and war follow. On a personal level, we tend to experience loneliness, depression, and anger. However, there is an alternative. When we remember the true nature of ourselves and each other, we may be able to let go of much of our mental pain—feelings such as self-hatred, self-judgment, and self-criticism—and experience genuine, egoless love toward ourselves and others. That love can heal all our wounds. Imagine what that world would be like. We would have much more awareness. We could even develop a more thoughtful way of relating to our natural world. Today we see the consequence of holding the natural world as an unlimited resource here for us to use at will for our comfort and enrichment. It is devastating. We are paying a huge price because we have been exploiting the natural world. We are jeopardizing the future of generations to come. Everything we do that is harmful to nature comes from not remembering that our world is intrinsically sacred.

In contrast, many Native American traditions have the view that everything in nature is sacred. When they take the life of an animal for food, they take that life with reverence. They perform a conscious ceremony honoring that animal and thanking them for giving their life to sustain human life. In the same way, many Tibetans pray before taking the life of an animal for food. Before eating meat, they offer prayers for the animal. Basically, they understand that the animal is equally important and precious. In the modern world animals are mass-produced like inanimate objects in huge factories, and we have forgotten that we are not different from them. As humans we seem to forget that each animal is vital, alive, and wants to be happy. We forget that each of them wants to live and that they can experience fear and terror when they are treated harshly. Maybe there is a way to use natural resources and a way to find a source of food while maintaining a reverence for life.

As human beings, not only do we forget to recognize that all living beings are sacred; we also forget the sacredness of our own being. Throughout history, over and over again, we humans forget that every group of people, every gender and every race, is equal, the same in the sense that all have the same divine nature. All need to be treated with respect and dignity. We can make a promise or a vow to constantly remember that everything is sacred. The world is sacred. All living beings, each human being that you meet, is sacred. All want to be happy, and all deserve that opportunity. Everybody and everything is equally sacred. There is no hierarchy in sacred. No one is more sacred than another. This is an important point to remember.

The true meaning of sacredness is the subjective experience that you feel wholehearted respect and reverence toward somebody or something and no longer harbor any intention to objectify. Today lots of people shun the notion of sacredness with the misconception that it is only a religious sentiment. This misconception has its root in two factors. One is that many organized religions proclaim a monopoly on "sacredness," and that forces people into the belief that they have to subscribe to a certain religious sect in order to have access to it. Another factor is the belief that there is an intrinsic duality between the spiritual and the secular, so people who identify as secular will close their minds to anything called sacred, and while they may feel that they just reject a religious doctrine, they may also shut the door to this spiritual and profound experience within themselves.

While growing up in Tibet I was raised in a culture where people go to the temples to bow to the images of buddhas and bodhisattvas. Every family has a shrine at home, no matter how wealthy or poor they may be, and they light candles, burn incense, and offer food and water to those images. You often feel that those temples and statues are sacred, yet Buddhism is a nontheistic religion and does not teach idolatry. Yet those practices teach people how to feel sacredness. The point is that experiencing sacredness should not stop at the shrine but expand to all things, including the natural world and all beings in it. The sacred is much simpler than what we think; it's all about respecting and embracing and not objectifying.

Objectifying is perhaps one of the oldest negative human habits. We often objectify people, and it is very destructive. To objectify means to degrade to the status of a mere object. To objectify is to deny the value and living presence in someone or something. We objectify people, and we objectify nature. We exploit both to fulfill our needs and desires. We think that nature is something we can simply use rather than protect and treasure as a precious resource. In the same way, we objectify each other. It can be quite shocking when we realize that we do this much of the time. We objectify each other not with intention but because we lack awareness in that moment. We do it unconsciously all the time. The moment we relate to somebody as a person with a nationality, a gender, or a specific personal history different from our own, we are objectifying that person. We are not recognizing that fundamentally we are the same. We are related; we are human beings; we share humanness.

When we say *humanness*, there is no obvious religious meaning. Yet humanness itself is sacred, timelessly sacred. When we are able to recognize humanness in everybody, then we can somehow see that there is sacredness in each person too. When somebody has caused us a great deal of pain sometime in our life, or when we find someone challenging, we often think of them as unlovable. We sometimes forget to open our heart and recognize the humanness in them. The moment we see humanness in such a person, we are able to embrace, we are able to forgive—we are able to love. We are able to love our worst adversary. Then we may feel less fear, mistrust, enmity and are more connected and the much-used phrase of *human brotherhood* or *sisterhood* will become a living experience. Until then those phrases are just some flowery concepts that mean nothing.

In the late nineties, a small group of us took a pilgrimage to Arizona and New Mexico in the USA and camped out at a few different sites such as Canyon de Chelly. It is one of those places that takes your breath away—you might call it a smaller version of the Grand Canyon. A lady from the Navaho tribe accompanied us as a guide. We did a Tibetan Buddhist practice called *chod*, which means "cutting through ego-clinging." During the trip I offered a talk to the group every day. The Navaho woman overheard the discourse while she was busy doing her chores nearby. One time I was talking about the Tantric Buddhist notion that everything is sacred. Toward the end she approached me and said that these ideas were similar to what her tradition teaches and is called "walking in beauty." In my understanding, walking in beauty entails being in harmony with the people of the world and all living things. It also signifies internal wholeness, a feeling that we are no longer fragmented and we have a benevolent relationship with the universe. Seeing the sacredness in everything is a way through which we can experience such goodness.

Albert Einstein said, "I think the most important question facing humanity is, 'Is the universe a friendly place?'" This question may seem very lofty to someone who lives from day to day and never ponders things like this. Einstein gave his own conclusion to this question—he concluded that yes, the universe is friendly, and we should use our attention and technology to try to understand it and build safety for all.

This question about the friendliness of the universe is important for everyone to think about. Whatever answer we come up with will have great impact on our subjective experience of our life. We could say that the universe is unfriendly. From one angle the cosmos seems extremely violent with supernovas and black holes, which devour everything. There are planetary catastrophes such as extinction through meteor impacts and volcanic eruptions, tsunamis, earthquakes, and extreme weather events. Our finite lifespan on earth is riddled with disease; struggle; and interpersonal conflicts and unending suffering because of poverty, war, and famine. From another angle we can find thousands of reasons to feel that the universe is a friendly place. It seems that our brain is wired to look at things from a more fatalistic perspective. Einstein pointed out that thinking that the universe is unfriendly has negative consequences for both individuals and the world as a whole. The only positive way to proceed is to decide that the universe is friendly. Maybe one of the ways to decide that both the universe and life on earth are friendly is to say that everything is sacred. Deciding the opposite would lead to either destruction or meaninglessness.

Tantric Buddhists have known all along how important a sacred outlook is, and they have used this in many visualizations and spiritual practices throughout history. They have been outspoken against sexism and the caste system. They took vows or commitments not to disparage women, because women often were not treated as equally sacred. Throughout its long history Tantric Buddhism has been teaching sacred outlook, which includes everyone, no matter what race, gender, or species. Buddhists also practice sacred outlook for the natural world. For them the trees, mountains, and all the elements are sacred. To practice this, they take our aversion to so-called unclean substances, such as excrement, and offer those in Tantric rituals to the divine in order to have a direct experience of sacred outlook and not just live in the world of concepts.

If humanity would come together and truly embrace a sacred outlook, many of our troubles would be over. We would be able to respect each other regardless of race, culture, religion, or social standing, and we would also revere the natural world and take care of it instead of exploiting and destroying it. In 2016 the Center for Interfaith Relations, a nonprofit organization, sponsored an interfaith gathering in Louisville, Kentucky. It was attended by representatives of all the major religions of the world. I was invited to speak. There was a true kinship among everyone there—Muslims, Hindus, and Christians. My heart felt elated and joyous walking in that beauty. At one point at an evening concert a bluegrass band from Kentucky joined musicians from Pakistan, and the outcome was delightful. It was a living metaphor for humanity coming together to create something truly beautiful. Let's remind each other to recognize each other's sacredness and become happier creatures.

8

humility, surrender, and devotion

There are a great variety of profound and beautiful spiritual teachings that are expressions of human wisdom. They are like different kinds of music, different flowers. The Tibetan traditions, for example, have created profound and beautiful spiritual teachings and practices. One, in particular, refers to the taste or flavor of something, and the Tibetan expression can be translated as "having an equal flavor or the same taste." Learning how to live in such a way that every experience has an "equal flavor" is the most difficult thing to experience and realize in this human life, but if you can realize it, it is also the secret and the beginning of true happiness, which is not dependent on external circumstances.

We often experience joy and happiness, but most of the time such feelings are conditional. That means they depend on causes and external conditions. For instance, we just had a delicious, sweet chocolate a few minutes ago, and that's why we are happy. Sometimes we don't need a lot of things to be happy for a while. We can go to a store like 7-Eleven and buy something very cheap and be very happy for a while. That happiness may last for a few minutes. Other times we are happy because we tell ourselves this wonderful story that something is going well in our life. This often happens when we feel that we have security, something to hold on to in life. When we receive a lovely card on our birthday, then we are very happy for a while. Sometimes we are happy when we have a change in our life, like a job promotion. But this happiness is based on outside circumstances, which are often transitory and can change at any given moment. Usually our happiness as a result of these situations is not lasting.

A few years ago a friend of mine taught me the expression "moving up in the world." Probably many of us have experienced the thought that we were moving up in the world, perhaps because we bought a new vacuum cleaner or a new toothbrush. When that happens, we can be almost ecstatic for a few minutes or, if we are really lucky, maybe for half an hour. We may also be doing spiritual practices such as meditation, yoga, or even Buddhist-oriented meditations to quiet our mind and help us feel joy and wellness. This is very good, something that we should welcome, but those practices may not make us happy in the ultimate sense. In my tradition, the Tibetan tradition, they say that the only way you can be happy in the true sense is to experience this thing called equal taste. How does that sound? It might not sound interesting if you are going to a restaurant. We don't want to experience equal taste at a restaurant.

This phrase "equal taste" is an analogy of course, an analogy used to describe a profound, extraordinary experience that we can all have access to. It is an experience of some kind of equanimity in which we are no longer lost in our hopes, fears, anger, or anxiety. We are no longer reacting to life's situations. We are simply embracing whatever is unfolding in front of us. We are experiencing something like all situations as having the same flavors, the same taste. It's almost like we are experiencing that the taste of death is the same as the taste of birth. It's almost like the taste of losing our possessions is the same as the taste of gaining this and that. When we experience this, it means that we are no longer lost in our preferences, no longer lost in this trap of fear and expectations.

In my tradition, they say that this equal taste is pretty much the only secret to absolute, unconditional happiness. Until we experience that, we will not know what unconditional happiness is. All of our happiness and joy is transient, changeable, and reversible until we know how to access this state of our own consciousness. Sometimes we might think, "Oh, it would be really nice to know this thing called equal taste." Then we try to practice meditation and all kinds of techniques, hoping that someday we can understand the equal taste that Tibetan teachers talk about.

Personally, as many of you know, I have been walking the spiritual path for many, many decades. I have learned from personal experience that you cannot force yourself to be liberated. It is not an easy endeavor. I feel I am a new student rather than a master in this field. It is a lifelong journey that humbles me again and again. What you need is some kind of surrender, humility, and devotion. You have to have an open heart, a heart open to something greater than your own ego, your own personality.

The idea of opening the heart beyond your own self reminds me of a rather ordinary event that happened not so long ago. I was flying to a meditation retreat I was leading, and I happened to open the shade on the airplane window to an amazing sight. The plane was flying above a thick layer of white clouds, and the sun was reflecting off those beautiful clouds. It was glorious, and I was very moved. I felt an amazing, heart-opening devotion to the beauty of the world and the beauty of existence. I also felt a powerful feeling of devotion to Tara, a female buddha. In the Mahayana tradition Tara symbolizes universal compassion. Tara is not outside; she is within each of us. She is a symbol of the universal compassion that lies at the core of our being. I felt such incredible inspiration and devotion that I wrote a poem or hymn in Tibetan to Tara, the embodiment of the divine. When I went back and read the poem that I had composed, I recognized that this was the true voice of my own heart. There is a lot of surrender in the poems that I write! Basically, in these hymns I recognized that sometimes I can't liberate myself; I can't enlighten myself. I can't force myself to experience this thing called equal flavor, equal taste that is the secret of unconditional happiness. So I was praying to Tara to please help me overcome all of my inner resistance and help me experience this awakened mind that realizes the same flavor or equal taste.

Perhaps many of you use prayer in your life. You don't have to be religious to pray. Prayer is an act of surrendering and trusting something much bigger than your own ego, bigger than your own personal will. When you read Tibetan spiritual liturgies, you find that they are filled with aspirations and prayers. "May I experience this equal flavor." We may need to use inquiry to find out what our resistance to experiencing this equal flavor, this equal taste is.

There are many extraordinary mystics, *mahasiddhas* such as the Tibetan yogi Milarepa, who live in this spirit of equal flavor. There is a story about a Zen master who was meditating near a village. In this village, a young woman had an affair with a young man and she got pregnant and gave birth to a child. But having a child out of wedlock was shameful in her culture, and she couldn't really tell anyone who the father of the child was. Finally, she said that the monk was the father of her child. He was an easy target; perhaps she felt safe with him. Her family and all of the people of the village approached the monk and said, "Oh, we thought that you were a noble being, but you are not. This is your child." The monk didn't try to argue or clarify. He said, "Is that so?" He took the child and became an amazing, kind, and responsible father, dedicating all of his time and effort to taking care of the child. Some years passed, and the woman finally had the courage to tell the truth. She told everybody that the father of the child was somebody else. Her family and all of the villagers became very excited. They went to the monk and said, "We are so sorry. We made a mistake. Now we are going to take the child away from you." This would be very painful for someone who has been taking care of a child and developed a close affinity with them. The monk didn't resist. He said, "Is that so?" This famous anecdote points out the extraordinary inner freedom of a freed consciousness in which all conditions, all circumstances are the same. We no longer have preferences. We no longer have fear and expectations.

What is the resistance to having such inner freedom? When we look inside, we often find a deep-seated desire to have complete control over our life. This ingrained impulse governs our everyday life and our relationship with world. The truth is that we do have limited control over our life. For example, tonight you can cook anything you want for dinner, and when you go to the store, you have choices, you can buy this or that. It may seem that we have a lot of control over our life. We have a choice about who we are going to be with, who we are not going to be with. We can decide what we are going to wear. We can choose to continue sitting, or we can get up and dance ecstatically. Ultimately, however, we don't have control of our life. For instance, we have no control over our death. Someday we are all going to die. We don't know when we are going to die, but we all know intellectually that we are going to die. Not one human being in all of our history has been able to escape death. Everyone dies eventually. If we live a long life, then we are going to age. We have no control over our aging. We have no control over our bodies. We don't know when we are going to get sick. We also don't know what event we are going to confront within even the next few hours. Anything can happen in our life in the next few hours. Life is always reminding us that we don't have absolute control over anything.

Every morning when we wake up, we may want to remind ourselves that we have no absolute control over our life and, in spite of that, welcome the day with an open heart. We may want to remind ourselves that we are going to invite the whole day with an open heart and with courage, even though we don't know what we are going to encounter. We may encounter beautiful, pleasant surprises, or we may go through tragedy, even catastrophe. Somehow we are living under this illusion that we can control life, and whenever we feel that we are losing control over our life we feel anxiety and anger. We are challenged and shaken to our very core.

It might be wonderful if we all prayed now and then. Prayer is a very powerful method. It is a means of inner liberation. Sometimes prayer is our last resort. If we have been walking the spiritual path, trying to become awakened, there may come a point when we realize that we can't force ourselves to experience this thing called equal flavor. Then prayer is our last resort. Prayer is an act of surrendering and opening our heart, trusting something that is much greater than our own personality, our ego.

There is a deep impulse in each of us that knows how to pray. We don't have to recite traditional prayers. We can all compose our own prayers. Did you ever have the experience when you were in trouble or when you were confused, that you naturally started praying? Maybe you didn't know that you were praying. Maybe you didn't have any concept of who you were praying to. There are some traditions where you have someone divine or sacred that you pray to. There are other traditions, nontheistic traditions, where you pray but you are not praying to anybody. When we are struggling with anything in our consciousness, we can always pray, remembering that we don't have to be religious or Buddhist to pray. We can ask the universe, "May I have the readiness to overcome my fear." Or if we are struggling with resentment, we can pray to the universe to help us overcome that. Praying to the universe is a very safe thing to do. We can ask the universe to bestow a shower of blessings on us and help us to overcome our inner demons of resentment, fear, and anger.

In the act of prayer, you can feel yourself surrendering all your hopes and fears, and you are freed from your resistance to accepting that you have no control in life. You feel true humility, in which you're no longer trying to be in charge, but letting life itself be in charge. Let yourself recognize that this is the highest freedom you can have. Try to live that freedom every day as much as you can. There will be moments in your life when you will feel that you don't need that freedom, but as humans we are going through ups and downs, and in some moments freedom will be the only refuge you have. We human beings are extremely resilient and strong—we have the capacity to be openhearted and to surrender in any situation. It is our innate potential. Let's use it.

9

a simple mantra

In one of the poems of a revered Tibetan saint, it says,

When your belly is full, you act like a spiritual person.
But when unfavorable conditions befall you, you become
very mediocre.

Usually there is the sense that when you are a spiritual person, you
are compassionate, wise, and courageous. This is not challenging
when conditions are going well for us. But it is another story when
things are not going our way.

There are two kinds of circumstances or conditions: one is favorable, and one is unfavorable. Even though conditions, intrinsically,
are neither favorable nor unfavorable, as human beings we tend
to perceive some events or conditions as favorable and then other
conditions as unfavorable. Sometimes what we perceive as unfavorable initially becomes very favorable sometime in the future.
For example, perhaps many of us have heard the story of the man

whose son was born blind. Everyone considered his blindness to be an unfortunate situation. But then, when the son grew up, there was a war and all of the young men had to join the army. But the blind son did not have to. He was allowed to stay home with his father. Then everyone thought his blindness was a fortunate condition. Conditions are like that. As we encounter them, we don't really know whether they will ultimately be fortunate or unfortunate.

For that reason, I often encourage people to practice gratitude. We can practice gratitude toward our parents or those who raised us, toward our friends, and toward other people who have showered us with kindness or done something beneficial for us at some time in our life. Also, when we wake up in the morning, we can be thankful for the day, for the sun. Every time we have a meal, we can practice gratitude too. There are many reasons to be grateful.

However, I also encourage people to practice gratitude for the trouble that they have in life. This is, of course, a little bit hard to relate to sometimes. Some of us may have had problems, troubles in our life, things that were very difficult to work with. Then later we realized that those troubles and problems were in fact a blessing in disguise. Even though at the time they were not very pleasant, we learned a lot from them. For one thing, we learned how to be compassionate and how to be courageous. I am sorry for the bad news, but as human beings we seem to need a few problems. Maybe there is some wonderful place in the universe where we don't have to go through any troubles, because from the moment we are born, we simply begin to evolve naturally into compassionate, wise, and courageous people. However, in this world it is almost a law of nature that as human beings we have to go through pain, heartache, challenges, and difficulties in order to truly grow and evolve, in order to become truly compassionate and wise. From that perspective, we can become thankful even for the conditions that we initially perceived to be very unfavorable and negative. Maybe at the time, we prayed that those conditions would go away quickly. Then later we expressed gratitude because we realized that because of that problem we grew. Because of it, we learned to be truly happy inside.

One of the first contemplations taught by Buddha was about remembering that everything in this life is impermanent. We use this contemplation or meditation to teach ourselves that all of the good circumstances are impermanent, so we should not be attached to them. For example, right now we might have good health, but we cannot get attached to that because that wonderful condition is not permanent. Eventually our good health will go away. Everything that we perceive as favorable is intrinsically impermanent. We cannot hold on to comfort, security, or any other favorable situation. We have to remind ourselves that their true nature is impermanent, and we have to let go of attachment to them. This reflection is designed to remind us of that. We have to be prepared. We have to be ready ahead of time. While we are mindful of that we can also use this contemplation to remember that all unfavorable circumstances are impermanent too.

There is a fable that reminds me of Buddha's teaching on impermanence. In this fable, there was a powerful king. He summoned all of his ministers and challenged them to search the kingdom for a magical ring he had heard about. The ring was magical because, in its presence, a sad person became happy immediately. All of his ministers searched high and low, but they could not find the ring.

One minister, as a last resort, went to the market and found an old silversmith. He asked the old silversmith if he knew of this magical ring. Miraculously, the silversmith had not only heard of the ring. He had one! The minister was amazed and asked to see it. The silversmith opened an old, dusty box, picked up a ring, and presented it to the minister. The minister looked at it and saw that it was inscribed with a simple phrase, "This too shall pass." The next day the minister went to the palace and presented the ring to the king, who was having a very elaborate banquet. The king looked at the ring and suddenly started crying. No one knew why he was crying. Then after a few minutes he startled giggling and laughing so hard that it made everyone else laugh.

This fable reminds us of Buddha's teaching on impermanence. It tells us that all events in life, all circumstances, are impermanent. They are transient; we cannot hold on to them. So, we might like to use the phrase, "This too shall pass." It can remind us of impermanence. We can use it as a mantra that we can chant now and then as a reminder. This does not mean that we should not be happy. We should be happy. But the phrase reminds us that we should not take refuge in the favorable conditions that we might be enjoying right now. This phrase reminds us that whatever we are attached to right now may not last forever

The ancient masters tell us that life's conditions are totally unpredictable in two different ways. What we are experiencing right now can change at any moment. In addition to that, we don't know what is on the way in the future. We don't know what the universe, in the grand scheme of all things, has in store for us. This is why we always have to be ready to respond to the new circumstances, challenges, surprises, and blessings that might be on the way. Sometimes big changes take place in our lives. These changes sometimes totally and completely challenge us. When we are not ready sometimes even small changes and events can completely throw us off balance. When we are more mindful of impermanence, we can get through the rough patches more easily.

When I was in South Korea in the fall of 2017, I was given a very special gift. It was a beautiful flower made out of fabric. It was made by mothers who had lost children due to a tragic accident a few years earlier. Perhaps you remember the news that in 2014 more than three hundred people—many of them children—drowned when the ferry they were on accidently sank in the ocean. Strangely, the first time I went to Korea, my visit coincided with that accident. At that time there was anger everywhere, even in the eyes of the people on the street who had not lost children themselves. I was scheduled to give a talk, but people were in such pain that I felt it was improper for me to speak. All I could do was sit in silence and hear their sorrow and pain. Now, three or four years later, it was clear that there had been healing. There had been wonderful closure. When I picked up the flower made by those mothers, I felt lots of pain, but I also felt this amazing closure. They had decided to let go of their anger. They learned how to turn their grief, their anger, and their sorrow into compassion and understanding. So, healing happened. Can you imagine such an event happening to you? How could you handle it? How would you respond? Probably none of these mothers and fathers expected that this was going to happen to them. Perhaps they couldn't believe it when they were told of the loss of their most beloved ones. What I am trying to say is that not only will our favorable conditions change, but in addition we don't know what is waiting for us. We don't know our future.

In my spiritual lineage, we are taught to meditate. We meditate again and again on this notion of impermanence taught by Buddha twenty-five hundred years ago. We keep meditating and meditating until that wisdom becomes part of our consciousness, and somehow this awareness is always within each of us. We know that nothing is permanent. We can enjoy the favorable conditions we are enjoying right now, but we also know that we should not get attached to them. We are aware that at any time we may be struck by devastating circumstances that we are not expecting.

If we don't have any kind of spiritual training in the form of contemplation, mindfulness, or reflection, even a small change in conditions or circumstances can sometimes totally challenge us. When I first came to this country, I was under the impression that everything was perfect here. The world looked very good. Then I heard about an incident of road rage. Someone cut another person off on the highway and that produced this amazing level of anger. The person got a gun and actually shot the other person. Why? Why is getting cut off on the highway such a big deal? So what? Maybe the other person had an urgent meeting or had to use the bathroom. Who knows? Maybe they were having such a good time they didn't notice they were cutting someone off. If we are not abiding in awareness, if our mind is not trained in mindfulness, then it is very easy to overreact. We all have habits of anger, fear and aggression in our psyche. Some of them are so deeply rooted that they are associated with our neurological and biological systems. Perhaps you know the concept of fight-or-flight. The more we reinforce our negative reactive patterns, the stronger they become, and our biological triggers are more frequently and violently reactivated. Aggressive and violent behavior can become almost instinctual. The person who shot somebody because of a road incident was perhaps acting from this instinctual behavior, almost like a caveman walking around with a club. When we are not mindful, we can easily overreact and suddenly become this wild beast as a result of even a slight change in circumstance. The truth is that we are sometimes reacting as if our situation was a major crisis rather than simply a small challenge.

There are two trainings we can use to overcome our overreactions. We can reflect on impermanence. Perhaps we can recite this phrase, "This too shall pass." We might like to recite this phrase now and then in our everyday life as a sacred offering. We can also practice self-awareness. We can become aware of our negative habits. We can see that in the structure of our consciousness there is a heap of old habits that are destructive and no longer useful. This is not personal. We all have these old, unexamined habits. But some people are not aware of them, and when there is no awareness, we have the potential to cause harm to other people, to our environment, and even to life itself. Awareness of these patterns and habits comes into being through deep contemplation and meditation practice.

Of course, we have to be mindful of danger, but we don't have to be overly cautious, alert, and reactive. We don't need to respond like we are walking on land mined with booby traps. We want to counter this kind of overreaction. We can do this by having some self-awareness every day and by constantly remembering that we have this heap of habitual patterns in our psyche sometimes triggering our neurological and biological systems to overreact. Being mindful of this, we can remember not to meet people and events from these overreactive places.

We have a choice not to respond to expressions of reality from our old habits. We can respond from a whole different dimension of consciousness. We can do this, and, in the end, we can experience amazing peace. We can come to a place in our life that is spoken about by great masters of many traditions. We can come to feel that all of the events of our life, all of the conditions of our life, are friendly to us. That is an amazing insight! All conditions become friendly to us, even the difficult ones. Even illness becomes friendly to us. This means that in the end we feel deep peace in the presence of all of the expressions of reality.

All conditions becoming favorable to us is not a concept. It is a beautiful human experience. It is not an epiphany, a transcendent experience, or a spiritual awakening. It is just an ordinary, beautiful, human experience that we can all have if we are willing. We can wake up and realize that we are not in total command of our life, and therefore we have to learn and prepare to keep surrendering and surrendering to whatever happens. We can remember not to close our heart. Sometimes when life becomes a little difficult or when somebody cuts us off on the highway, we close our heart. That is our biggest danger because the human heart wants to open. The human heart has a natural desire to open and with it there is a sweet surrender, a surrender to life. There is compassion, forgiveness, and acceptance and we are no longer lost in a state of mind that is filled with old habits. We are in another dimension of mind and consciousness in that very moment.

10

going beyond self-image

*M*any people traveled to the East in the 1960s and 1970s and explored various Buddhist traditions and yogic disciplines. An American spiritual teacher studied with many masters in the East during those days. When people asked him what he learned from all of the masters, his answer was rather unusual. He told them what they *didn't* they teach him rather than what they *did* teach him. He would say, "None of them teach to cling." This is a brilliant answer. He knew how to point out the quintessence of all of the spiritual teachings. In other words, he didn't miss the point. The heart of many of these ancient teachings is the notion of nongrasping. There are many ways this timeless wisdom can be applied. We can embody nongrasping in everyday life when we encounter a variety of situations that just happen to us when we are not expecting them, when we were, in fact, expecting something else. We can practice nongrasping simply by accepting the new occurrence, without grasping to what we were expecting.

Nongrasping can be practiced in relation to our material acquisitions and possessions. We can get very attached to what we own and also to what we want. We can become very lost in these things. We can also apply the principle of nongrasping to our concepts, ideas, and beliefs. We often become really attached to these, even though they are nonmaterial and insubstantial. One of the most powerful attachments that we are all dealing with, without even knowing it, is our attachment to self. This is called *self-grasping*, and it is an extremely powerful attachment. Many people are unhappy and suffer painfully in this world because they are attached to what we can call their self-image.

We walk around with an image in our head about who we are. Yet this self-image is totally false; this self-image is not who we really are; this self-image is not born with us. We never meet a newborn child who has a concept about who he or she is. Infants do not have any self-images. That's why a newborn child is enlightened in some way. They are mystical transcenders in many ways because they don't yet have an ego structure and obviously they don't have any kind of self-image in their mind. However, as time goes by, everybody develops a sense of personal self and they go through the process of developing very strong self-images.

Like newborn children, animals also have no self-image, and they also do not project anything onto you. That's the reason we feel so relaxed and comfortable around our pets. They love us unconditionally no matter how we look or what we are going through at the time. They never criticize us as a loser or as dumb.

In human development, it is natural to go through the stages from no ego structure, or born without any concepts in pure innocence, to a fully matured ego with a strong self-image. This self-image is so strong that we end up believing that this is who and what we are. In the next stage, we are supposed to outgrow all self-images and arrive at the authentic version of ourself. It is very hard to challenge these layers of self-image because they are constantly being reinforced by the standards, values, and perceptions of the culture we live in.

Yet we must question the foundation of the self-image that we are all so very attached to. Every one of us has their own self-image or self-images and we are totally identified with them, attached to them. But self-image is purely a mental construct. It is an imaginary edifice. A product of our mind, our imagination. It does not exist anywhere else. It obviously does not exist outside of us; it does not exist anywhere inside of us either. It is a fictitious entity that only exists as pure imagination. Yet people suffer tremendously by being attached to their self-image. They suffer from pride, from guilt, from self-loathing, from shame, and from feeling that they are inadequate or unattractive. Many people are constantly battling with feeling that they are not good enough or not intelligent enough. They feel that they don't have enough money or that they haven't achieved enough. There are cultures in our modern world where people are literally battling a psychological epidemic of self-loathing and self-doubt. In some countries, a huge percentage of the population feels that they are intrinsically imperfect. This is especially true in our relationship with our bodies. Some people don't like the way they look to the extent that they go through extreme plastic surgery in order to completely reconstruct their facial structure. Others starve or otherwise harm themselves out of a sense of inadequacy. This is happening in some modern cultures, and in many ways, it is quite sad.

We can also feel that we are not intelligent enough or that we haven't achieved enough in our lives. We haven't met our career or

71

academic ideals. We can also feel that we haven't accumulated the wealth and fortune that we should have. We don't have enough of this or enough of that. We have developed these negative self-images in our mind, and we can sometimes be extremely harsh on ourselves. We judge and criticize ourselves. We can conclude that there is something wrong with us, and therefore we are not lovable.

On the other hand, we can develop pride, thinking that somehow we are better than others, more intelligent than others. We can think that we have achieved things that most other people haven't achieved. When we think this way, we can develop pride. Pride is very painful too. Usually at the very heart of this pride, there is guilt, shame, and even self-loathing. There is no pure pride, pride that is as pure as gold. All forms of pride are mixed with guilt and shame; all of them are poisoned. This is why Buddha said that if you think you are better than anybody else, you are deluded. And if you think that you are worse than others, you are also deluded. If you think you are equal to others, you are still deluded. Pride, guilt, and thinking that you are equal to others all come from the fact that we are comparing ourselves with others.

There are many people who are quietly suffering due to psychological issues related to self-image. Often this is not caused by individual neuroses—rather, this suffering is almost superimposed by the conventional environment they are exposed to. The image of what is considered to be good-looking is very specific, and those standards are indoctrinating people at a very early age. Childhood toys such as Barbie dolls and characters in Disney movies superimpose powerful images on young children. They imprint standards that cause poor self-images for many young girls and specifically for minority groups such as people of color. Qualities like beauty are dependent on our perception and have no absolute definition. As the saying goes, "Beauty lies in the eyes of the beholder."

Recently I read an article about a young black girl. This young lady had a terrible experience while attending kindergarten. She was bullied because of the way her hair and skin looked. But this did not discourage her, and she decided to take action so that all black and brown girls could feel beautiful. She started to collect dolls of all skin colors and gave them away for Christmas. So far, she has been able to distribute twenty thousand dolls in the United States, Haiti, and Africa. She is now eleven years old. This is an inspiring story. Perhaps we can also take action to challenge some of our own preconceived ideas about what is beautiful. Our ideas are often one-dimensional and invalid, and they have the potential to harm us and others.

These self-images that we create in our lives have to be questioned. Until we start questioning them, there is no true spiritual development, no true awakening. True transformation requires that we question and challenge our self-image. That is why this questioning is an important part of the spiritual journey. It is useful to develop a practice of questioning and inquiring into the self-image that we are holding on to. First, we must question how we even constructed our self-image in the first place. We might like to question its components, its makeup and building blocks. We are not born with such concepts, so where did they come from? Sooner or later we learn that the self-image that we are all identified with actually comes from ideas and beliefs about who we are. They are ideas and beliefs that we invented as well as ideas and beliefs that have been given to us by the people and society around us. It is from these two factors that we create this mental edifice that we are then very stuck with. In the end, we come to the realization that all forms of self-image are not real. They are illusory. They are not who we really are. How do we get to that understanding?

There are some radical traditional Buddhist practices for dealing with our self-image. One practice is this: You leave your home and travel around. You simply leave everything behind and carry only a small tent and walk about. You camp at a different site every time so you don't get attached to any particular place, because the moment you stay more than one or two nights in a spot, you start creating a sense of home. Then you start to think, "That's my bed." Even though there is no house, no bed, you start marking territory. "This is my territory; this is my home. This is where I am going to sleep to-night, and nobody should sleep here without my permission." Even though there are no buildings, our mind starts marking territory just like dogs sometimes do. We do that with our mind and who knows what else we will do if we stay more than one night in the same place? We claim things even in totally empty and strange places like the desert or the mountains. With this method of traveling around, we keep moving and therefore avoid staking false claims. This practice may not be practical for many people in modern life, but it can be illuminating to contemplate.

Another recommended Buddhist practice for cutting through self-image is to do things that counter the accepted behavioral norm. For example, you might live for a while as a yogi or wandering mendicant who has a carefree lifestyle. You stop trying to look good or be appealing to the outside world. This practice might not fit in with modern society either. In the old days, many great masters used this kind of unconventional and radical practice to be free from the confinement of self-concern. The idea is to radically drop all of your obsessions. You drop your vanity, your hope, your fear, and your concepts about right and wrong. Basically, you let go of trying to maintain your self-image. Instead, you destroy it. Many people, when they finish a practice like this, come out of the experience with an amazing freedom, an amazing sense of relief in their consciousness. They experience a feeling of rebirth in their consciousness since they died many times on their pilgrimage. What really died? What died are their concepts and their ideas of who they are. In some of the radical teachings of the masters, we are invited to experience a type of death. They are not talking about literal, physical death. They are talking but about an inner death, the death of every concept and every belief we have about who we are. In some sense, when you lose your self-image, you actually are dying. Your pride is dying along with shame and guilt. Your life's stories die together with your pain, sorrow, and hatred.

Every one of us is indeed this amazing being that is as mysterious as the universe itself. We are this amazing flow of energy that cannot be captured in a box of identity nor can it be solidified in any one way. Sometimes we can't even name who or what we are. Buddha taught that we are not a singular entity, rather we are a living conglomeration of many components that is constantly changing. As a human being, we are this indescribable, ever-flowing reality that has many dimensions. Not only that, all the dimensions that make up who we are, are constantly changing and morphing. They are dissolving and coming into being in each and every moment. So we are this ever-flowing, indescribable reality that we cannot really capture in one particular concept or idea.

There is a very beautiful inquiry that we can use to deconstruct our self-image. We can continually ask the question, "Who am I?" The inquiry is not unique to any one tradition. Masters in many traditions, including the Buddhist tradition, teach this method directly or indirectly. "Who am I?" The point of the inquiry is not so much to come up with an answer. Rather, it is a process through which we keep deconstructing and dissolving our self-image. We go about completely dissolving our self-image and along with that we dissolve our pride, our guilt, and our shame. We just deconstruct the whole thing, and then we wake up and see who we truly are. In the end, we might need to turn our attention inside and ask, "Who am I? What is self?" so that we can keep transforming and keep our identities dying inside. We can keep letting go of all of these concepts, all the very deep-seated ideas and beliefs about ourselves that we have been cherishing—all the concepts that create this painful illusion of who and what we think we are.

In modern pop psychology, there is an emphasis on developing a positive self-image. It results in many benefits. People have more self-confidence and better achieve their goals pertaining to the world, like their career or their relationships with other people. But this self-image is just an illusion that we conjure up in our mind and it is not what we truly are. It is a superficial remedy, just like a golden mask or a golden chain that imprisons you. As long as we have any kind of strong self-image in our mind either positive or negative, we are very subject to them and there is a lot of pain involved in maintaining such a self-image. If we truly want to be happy, we have to transcend all self-images. This is not an easy task. It is not for everybody. It is for those who have the strong desire to find this freedom that never can be lost.

In the ancient wisdom traditions, techniques have been developed that allow one to experience a state in which all such self-images are dissolving. For example, in Vajrayana practices, one visualizes oneself as an archetypal deity and holds a divine pride. This pride has nothing to do with ordinary pride; it is a method to release all self-images and rest in the source of your being, which is love and courage. Sometimes we are the closest to our self but also on the furthest frontier from it. Some people will be born and die continuously being locked up in the mental prison of their self-images, never finding out who they truly are.

11

invoking peace

There is much kindness, benevolence, and many acts of compassion in our human world. Sometimes we forget to recognize this wealth of goodness happening all the time around us. At the same time, we also have to acknowledge that there is a lot of pain, conflict, and misery happening every day as well. We see that much of the pain and misery around us is actually caused by the thoughts and the actions that we humans engage in. From that point of view, perhaps the best remedy to our problems is the ancient concept of *ahimsa*, a Sanskrit word that means "nonviolence." Ahimsa is one of the foundational practices of the great wisdom traditions of the East. Until there are enough people practicing ahimsa, we may not see any true fundamental change in our world. Of course, we will see a lot of superficial changes: changes in politics, in fashion, even changes in our attitudes and values. It seems that the world is constantly changing in many ways and yet the truly important change—the change of consciousness, the change of the mind and heart—will not actually happen until we have enough people in the world practicing ahimsa, nonviolence, with sincerity.

There was a movement in India around the time of Buddha called the *Sramana* movement. Those following Sramana traditions were ascetics, and one of their main practices was ahimsa. The Buddha is considered to be a great Sramana, a sage. Extraordinary sages and ascetics spread the movement of ahimsa throughout India and beyond. It went everywhere, into every culture in the form of a philosophy as well as a spiritual practice. There are many people who practice ahimsa even today. Yet we need more people practicing ahimsa.

We need a whole new movement, the ahimsa movement. Ahimsa can be a source of peace, harmony, and happiness for us as individuals as well as for the entire human family. There are a lot of movements happening in the world; some of them are good, and some of them are very questionable, not good, and maybe even harmful. The harmful movements sow mistrust, disharmony, anger, hatred, and even prejudice and bigotry. We should not be complacent, thinking that as humanity we are all evolved and don't really need to evolve anymore. We can't say, "Let's just relax. We don't have to worry about transforming the consciousness of humanity. It's already evolved. Let's not meditate. Let's just have fun. Let's eat more food. Let's use more resources. Let's have a good time. We don't have to meditate or worry about transforming our consciousness." This would be a form of complacency. Actually, we have to feel some kind of urgency. We all have to work together to transform our consciousness, the consciousness of all humanity. Not just yours and mine.

You may think that you are just one individual, and you really can't do much about the consciousness of all humanity when you are already having difficulty changing the consciousness of your brother or your sister or your troubled cousins. You may have been a great meditator, doing all these prayers and hoping that you could at least change the consciousness of your troubled cousin. Then you noticed that he is not changing at all. In fact, he's getting worse. We have every right to believe that we don't have anything to offer as a contribution to the human race. It's easy to be completely discouraged. However, just practicing nonviolence, ahimsa, can be the greatest contribution we can make to all humanity, this giant family of our human brothers and sisters.

Last Saturday I went to Big Sur with a group of people. We had to drive for a few hours to get there, and a friend of mine told me about his conversation with a scientist. It really got my attention. He said the scientist told him they have discovered this phenomenon that when you share a similar genetic makeup with a person or even a whole group of people—perhaps your relatives—even when you are living far away, maybe even on the other side of the world, those people can actually feel or even experience the emotions you are experiencing. This is a very interesting phenomenon. I don't know whether it is true or false, but I like the thought. Even if this is a false doctrine, perhaps we should consider it. Then we may wake up and realize that our anger is not just hurting us. It is also hurting a lot of other people, perhaps even our parents or other relatives. If we allow ourselves to be carried away by our own anger, we are also causing harm and suffering to them, to their consciousness. Maybe there is truth in that phenomenon.

The nonviolence taught by Buddha is the practice known as the four observances of Sramanas, or the four disciplines of the ascetics. Let me translate these four disciplines:

All the abused do not return abuse.
All those made angry do not respond with anger.
All those censured do not respond with criticism.
All those struck never strike back.

These four dharmas of Sramanas are considered the most basic and most elementary spiritual practice in the Buddhist tradition. When you look into these four disciplines, it's all about the practice of ahimsa, nonviolence. Nonviolence is how you respond to everything. Nonviolence begins in your mind and heart. Violence also begins in your heart and mind. Violence has many forms. It doesn't have to be some terrorizing act that we perform, like hurting a living being with a kind of barbaric behavior. Violence has many forms; it can be extremely subtle. That's why Shantideva said that when you look at others, remember to look at them with a loving expression. This is about not spreading even the slightest image of violence in your relationships, in your interactions with other human beings and other living beings. Or maybe you don't always look at everybody with a loving expression. It depends on where you live. There are some cultures where you can't really look at people with a loving expression; they may get paranoid and think you want something from them. They may run away from you. In addition to violence in how we look at others, when we look closely, we find violence in our speech all the time.

As I mentioned in a previous chapter, I was once leading a meditation retreat based on chod in Canyon de Chelly in Arizona. We had wonderful Native Americans guiding and protecting us. They were our guardians; they made sure that we were safe and that we knew how to get around. Finally, when we finished our retreat and came out of the canyon, we were talking about the kindness of these Native Americans. One person said that the tribe our guides belonged to have no curse words in their language. That's kind of amazing. Then she said that it might also be true in the Tibetan language because Tibetan culture is very spiritual. I was sorry to dispel this notion, but my language is full of curses and swearwords, more than any language I know, especially in the region called Golok where I come from. It is a small population, maybe a few hundred thousand people, but they managed to come up with a big treasury of curses and swearwords. Some of them are hilarious. I was translating some of the curses from my hometown into English. Some of them are actually humorous and some are not so humorous.

Even with this treasure trove of curses, there is a vow we take in Golok that I've never found in any other region in Tibet or in any other culture. I actually took that vow when I was young. As you know, Tibetans take all kinds of vows: spiritual vows, personal vows, a vow of vegetarianism, and so forth. Every tradition has a whole list of vows that you can take. But in my hometown, there is a vow not to swear, not to curse. Because perhaps people realize that every time you swear or curse, violence is already happening in your action and also in your consciousness. Because whenever we utter words, they are all coming from someplace in our consciousness. So, when we say words that are unkind, that somehow have the power to hurt someone's feelings, the violence, anger, and hatred have been reinforced in our consciousness, made more concrete, more established.

We can all be modern Sramanas and apply those four observances in everyday life. For example, when people challenge us, our usual impulse is to respond to them in an angry fashion or to get even with that person. Next time, when someone does something that challenges you, remember not to retaliate against them. Remember not to respond to their anger with anger, not to respond to their violence with violence. When you are abused, you are not supposed to return abuse. Abuse is not something we should let happen to anyone, including ourselves. There is a way to respond to stop the very act of abuse in a nonaggressive and intelligent way. We may run into everyday situations where people actually challenge us. That can be a form of violence or sometimes even abuse. People may challenge you all the time, without their intending to. I like the expression "to push somebody's buttons." You might like to visualize yourself as this being with a different body. Let's say you have a karmic body or a body of emotions, predispositions, and preferences. Then imagine that this body is like some kind of robot that has all these buttons. Remember, it is a simple visualization of your karmic body. It is not a very uplifting visualization, unlike that of your subtle body, which includes chakras, channels, and so on as taught in the Tantric traditions. They are very uplifting. The robot image is not inspiring, but it is effective.

So, you might like to periodically visualize your karmic body as some kind of robot that has many buttons. Visualize the button of passive-aggressiveness, the button of anger, the button of insecurity, the button of shame, the button of aggression. It seems the whole world is waiting to wake up so they can push your buttons. The only time that you would be really alone is when you are in deep sleep. Then you may feel the world and everybody has left; maybe that's why we are so attached to deep sleep. Everybody is really praising deep sleep these days. People really love it. They always ask, "Did you have a wonderful sleep last night?" Of course, it is good to have deep sleep because then we feel rejuvenated, we can think carefully. But maybe we love deep sleep because we feel, "Finally everybody left me alone last night. The whole world left me alone, right?" It feels that way.

Do you feel that way when you wake up early in the morning? You walk to your kitchen, maybe perhaps you make coffee. Many people do. Brush your teeth and just volunteer to stand in line to have your buttons pushed. There is a whole list of volunteers who have already signed up to push your buttons. Not only that, the whole world is interested in pushing your buttons and presenting all the things that really do that, like having a flat tire on the highway when you have to get somewhere on time. Maybe there is no more cell reception. That can push your button too, because you can't read your Facebook page anymore. How can you exist without Facebook? That existence would be terrifying. A world of anxiety, boredom, insecurity, restlessness. It seems that literally everybody wants to push your buttons, but the truth is that most of the time nobody wants to push your buttons. This is the truth. The world does not have any intention to challenge you. The world is just dancing. The world, life, whatever you like to call it, is always dancing.

The world is not dancing in accordance with our preferences, choices, likes, and dislikes. The universe is this amazing miracle that we can never comprehend, and it's always dancing. It does what it does. In many ways, whatever is happening even in this moment is actually that miracle. This dance, this cosmic dance of life, the world, and existence. We might like to use this beautiful Sanskrit word *lila*, the "divine play." We might actually like to regard everything that is happening in this moment as lila, a divine play, a divine dance.

So, let's say maybe somebody challenges you. It doesn't really matter whether this person is doing it with intention or completely unconsciously. Then we can tell ourselves, this might be an opportunity to practice ahimsa or the four disciplines of Sramana. That is, tell ourselves not to react. Not to react to challenges from unawareness, from anger, from aggression, from pure hatred, or from fear. Because the moment we react to the challenges being presented by people, the world, or life, we react from fear and hope, and the manifestation—what really comes out—is violence. Violence basically has the power to take us away from whatever we like to call our true nature, our buddha nature. It can destroy our peace, our happiness, and our love. Not only that, violence that we radiate, that we spread around in our environment, also has a toxic power to destroy the peace of others as well. Then violence actually feeds others' tendencies to act violently. Violence can spread like some kind of powerful poison that we cannot control easily.

Sometimes the violence of one person or even a small body of individuals has the power to trigger fear and anger in the consciousness of millions—a whole nation. A small body of individuals can say there is another group of people or another nation that presents a threat to our existence because this small body has seen some signs indicating such a threat to our existence. These people can actually spread so much fear, anger, and hatred in the hearts of millions and millions of people. Before you know it, they might even be contemplating the use of destructive weapons such as nuclear weapons. This kind of situation has happened many times throughout history. When there is the slightest sign that another nation or another group of people are somehow presenting a threat to our existence, then there are many cases where people are ready and willing to use destructive weapons like a nuclear bomb. We can easily lose awareness and love when we allow ourselves to be ruled by our unconscious tendencies and when we overreact to outside situations.

Love feeds love. This is good news. If you are able to remain in that state of nonviolence, then you exude loving-kindness and peace. That also goes everywhere, too. Your nonviolence somehow transforms the consciousness of others around you. Of course, you as a human being are a living bodhisattva; in many ways every human being is a living buddha. You are a living buddha who has the power to transform the consciousness of others. Even statues and sacred images can represent the buddha mind, the awakened mind, the mind of love and compassion, and have the power to transform the consciousness of other people. You may have heard the news a few years ago about an outdoor altar that was built in a public area in Oakland. The neighbors complained—they didn't want to have an altar outside in a public space. So, there was a meeting in the neighborhood, and the residents learned that since the shrine was placed in the neighborhood, the level of crime, violence, and domestic violence had dropped in a very remarkable way. So, they said, "Let's keep this altar." What was happening in my understanding was that this image, like images of Buddha and of Quan Yin, are amazing sacred representations designed as an allegory—these symbols that can invoke love and compassion and peace in everyone who sees them.

The truth is that you are more than a representation. You are more than just a sacred image. You are indeed a living buddha. Every human being is a living buddha. Some of us don't act like living buddhas, but that's something we have to accept. That's okay too. It is the very premise of the Mahayana tradition that every human being is a living buddha in themselves. So, you have the power to not only transform your consciousness, but also the consciousness of others.

There is a story about a monk, a wandering mendicant, who got very cold when the sun went down and night arrived. He knocked on everybody's door but couldn't find any place to sleep. Finally, he came across a monastery. He knocked on the door, but the monks didn't answer. He jumped the gate, went inside the main temple, and lay down, but he still felt extremely cold. He looked around and he saw a beautiful wooden statue of Buddha. He went to the altar, brought the statue down, and made a nice fire with it. The next morning the monks came to meditate and pray. They saw that their statue was gone. They looked around and saw this crazy mendicant sleeping in ashes, and they knew what had happened. The monks got furious and started yelling at him. Some young monks got really angry and started beating him. They said, "How can you do this? You performed blasphemy. You destroyed an image of Buddha." And he said, "I'm not the one who performed the blasphemy. You are. All I did was burn an image of Buddha, but I am the living buddha. You are abusing the real buddha." This is a very interesting story reminding us that every human being is a living buddha.

We each have many, many gifts, including the power to transform the consciousness of the whole world. The place to start is with the practice of nonviolence, the four disciplines of the Sramanas.

12

thank you to life

Sometimes the circumstances and events of our life remind us just how fragile human life can be. Now and then when we, or those close to us, have an accident or experience a sudden illness, we begin to wake up and realize how fragile and transient life is. Our ordinary, conventional world does not encourage us to reflect on the transient nature of our human existence. We usually have a comfortable attitude of unawareness or even denial most of the time in our everyday life. However, when we meditate, we focus on our interior life. We reflect on topics such as our birth, death, and the transient nature of our existence. We begin to recognize that our life is extremely rare and precious. We begin to cherish our life. We feel it is a gift, a great gift from the universe.

We feel this gift most strongly when we run into shocking circumstances like a sudden illness or a car accident. Then we often come to finally realize how impermanent and fragile our existence is. We are as fragile as a beautiful flower. When we hold a beautiful flower, we are careful not to hold it too tightly because it can be destroyed. It is like the dew on a blade of grass. It is extremely beautiful but unbelievably delicate. The great adept Nagarjuna said that he was amazed, even dumbfounded, every morning when he woke up and realized that he hadn't died in the night. To him it was a miracle that he was still here, still breathing.

In 2009 US Airways flight 1549 ran into trouble right after takeoff in New York, and the pilot was able to land the plane in the Hudson River. All 150 passengers on board survived the ordeal. Many people watched the event on television, and it became part of the American psyche. A movie based on this event was even made. Those passengers must have been excited beyond belief once they realized that they had escaped the jaws of certain death. They probably forgot all of their life's problems in that moment. Passengers reported in interviews that the event had a profound effect on how they looked at life. Hopefully we won't have to go through such an extreme experience in order to appreciate each moment of our life.

Even when there is no big tragedy, people can feel tormented by the drudgery of their life and they cannot find any joy in the repetition of their daily activities. They tend to think that drudgery originates from repeating chores to no end, but those same activities can be a source of fulfillment and joy when we embrace the moment we perform them. The rich joy of being alive can be found in doing those ordinary things, and it seems that we need to retrain our brain to learn to be joyous in doing ordinary things and in living each moment. The good news is that the brain is flexible.

When we are young we may feel like we are invincible, and it is especially difficult to feel the fragile and transient nature of our existence. Intellectually we know that we are going to die someday. Even though we know that death can sometimes be sudden and unpredictable, we feel that the actual day is sometime in the very distant future. We think that it will not arrive in the next few years or even in the next few decades. We live in this very comfortable denial. Somehow, even unconsciously, we believe that death is not close. We think that we are almost immortal. We think that we are too young to meditate on topics such as the transient nature of our own existence. Our grandmother and grandfather are old and may die at any moment, so it is important for them to contemplate these matters.

However, once we reach a certain age, we begin to wholeheartedly accept that our death is a truth that sooner or later we will all have to face. We may begin to feel a little uncomfortable with the fact that we are extremely fragile and our existence is going to fall apart eventually. Then finally we wholeheartedly accept the fact that our human life is transient, and a sense of gratitude, an amazing appreciation for our existence, spontaneously arises. We realize that we are very fortunate to have our life and we feel unconditional fulfillment and joy. We realize that we already have the most precious gift, our own life, and we sometimes feel an unbelievable joy simply because we are still breathing.

For many years I have been leading meditation retreats and giving talks at my community temple in Point Richmond, a quaint, historical town in the San Francisco Bay Area. Often after the talk there is a long greeting line of people who want to chat with me. Recently a gentleman approached me. When I asked how he was doing, he replied, "I am still breathing." That was a simple answer. He was not complaining. It was, rather, a spontaneous expression of his joy at being alive. You could see it in the twinkle of his eyes and the little smile in the corner of his mouth. Even though his answer was so simple, not a mind-blowing or profound answer, it left a strong impression on me.

This kind of spontaneous joy is spoken about in many traditions, and it has been expressed in many poems. But such joy does not happen all the time. We feel it when we reflect deeply and when our hearts are totally open. We especially feel it in those moments when we notice that our life is slowly and steadily passing away, and we remember how transient and precious all life is. We feel it when we set aside old concepts, our ego, our judgments, and mental strategies.

Some of us come to these realizations not through the circumstances or events of our life nor through prayer and reflection, but rather through what is often called a midlife crisis. We realize that time is running out, and we have not accomplished everything we hoped to accomplish. We have not fulfilled all of our dreams. We have not done all of the things that we planned to do, and now it is looking like we are running out of time. When people have a midlife crisis, they sometimes do very strange things. A man might buy a really nice red sports car. A woman might try something drastic to change her looks, to appear more youthful. When we fully accept the fact that our bodies are not immortal, we might start to feel a little anxiety. We may decide we are going to do things we've always wanted to do but haven't gotten around to yet. We want to totally cherish this life before it comes to an end. Sometimes we can become very spiritual because we want to have meaning, true meaning, in our life. We don't want to just survive every day. We want to contribute and do things that can help the world so we can feel that there is meaning in our life. Maybe we want to travel somewhere we haven't been. Maybe we want to push the boundaries a little bit so we can be excited and feel that we are living life fully as a result. An alternative way to handle the situation is to do something much more spiritual. We can pack our backpack and spend a few weeks or months hiking somewhere in nature, in the mountains or near the ocean. Someplace where we can fully appreciate nature.

Human life is sometimes very abstract because we think of it as a singular entity. Actually, human life has many components. Time is one component. We count our life in years. In order to have the year, we need the months, the weeks, the days and hours, and then the moments. If we don't pay attention to the present moment, then the life we are thinking about, the one we want to live fully, is actually just a mental construct. It is just an idea we have in our head. In order to cherish and embrace our human life, to live it fully, we have to begin to pay attention. Not to the year, because a year is too long. So is a month. We have to pay attention to this day, this very day; and not only to this very day but also to this very hour and this very moment. We can make a vow to cherish today. We should act now because once this day is gone, we cannot recreate it, we cannot relive it. Once this day is gone, it is gone forever. We cannot revisit it. We cannot bring back even one second from all the years that have already passed. So, this present moment is all we have. We might want to give it our full attention and really embrace it. To really live our life fully, we have to learn how to live in and embrace this moment.

The idea of embracing each moment is more than learning how to be in the present each moment. Accepting each moment requires us to face whatever situation unfolds with an open heart. It is about learning how to respond to all situations—the good ones and the not-so-good ones—with an open heart. It is a deep and rewarding spiritual practice. Life presents us with many opportunities to practice accepting each moment. Most of the time we cannot predict what situations we are going to face. Common sense may give us some clues. Most likely we have an idea of what is going to happen this afternoon. We don't know every detail, but we have a rough idea about what is going to happen. We know we are going to have dinner. We know we are going to go to bed. But sometimes we run into situations we didn't have a clue about. So, we don't really have absolute knowledge about what is waiting for us tomorrow or even this afternoon. That does not mean we should live with anxiety and fear. Actually, we should live with joy, with an open heart, with compassion, and with courage.

Some situations can only be met with courage and compassion. This is usually a time when we face a sudden catastrophe or some unknown future. If we can respond to an unexpected crisis or difficulty with courage, then we are able to accept and embrace that moment with an open heart. In addition to that, an amazing, powerful shift occurs in our consciousness, and we are changed in very profound ways. Our whole heart, our whole consciousness is transformed. We evolve, mature, and grow in a very dynamic direction.

We don't always have to respond to a challenging situation. Sometimes we have to respond to a situation with gratitude and appreciation because something very beautiful, comforting, benevolent, and auspicious has happened. There are many benevolent moments we should respond to with devotion and joy, and that's something we also have to learn. We don't always know how to respond to all the blessings and all the goodness in our lives with an open heart.

Sometimes we are too lost in our own mind to notice them. Then we do not see the many blessings and the many benevolent forces showering us here and there. We should remember to respond to those special moments with appreciation and gratitude, because sooner or later those moments will dissolve.

Perhaps you have had the experience of walking somewhere when unexpectedly you come across something so wonderful that the magic of existence just shocks your mind. Suddenly there is a beautiful sunset. The whole sky has turned into a bright orange color, and you realize that actually, this is magic. The sunset, this sacred manifestation, is the play of the universe. Sometimes you want to take a picture of it, but by the time you pick up your smartphone, it's already gone.

13

our heart already knows

We take on many identities in our life. We sometimes identify ourselves as secular rather than religious or spiritual. But the truth is that every human being is spiritual, whether or not they can accept that part of themselves. Some people are very happy to identify as spiritual, and others work very hard to deny that part of themselves. Every human being is spiritual because the strongest feeling or impulse we have is very spiritual. Our strongest impulse is our innate desire to become greater inside, to become selfless, and to experience transcendence. We want to become transcenders.

A few years ago, I had the opportunity to visit a Christian monastery, the Abbey of Gethsemani in Bardstown, Kentucky. Three monks from the monastery spent about two hours with me. We talked about many topics, and I felt great harmony and brotherhood with them. Of course, being monks, they didn't have any problems regarding their relationships, money, or marriage. All they wanted to talk about was transcendence. You don't run into many people who don't want to talk about problems with relationships, money, or politics, but all these monks wanted to talk about was transcendence.

They said that they were a little disappointed because they felt that today most people do not long for transcendence. Of course, that is their perception. They are talking about transcendence in their own religious context, in terms of becoming one or connecting with the divine. A few years ago, I visited a Zen monastery in France. A French Zen teacher there said he thought that not many people want transcendence these days. He said, "Everyone wants to live like Americans." I'll never forget that comment, though I'm not certain exactly what he meant.

For some people, transcendence means transcending our personal needs, or our ego, or our personal feelings. It means going beyond all of these through devotional, selfless love toward something much greater than ourself such as the divine, or God, and so forth. There are also people who don't have the perception of the divine, or God, and they are, perhaps, referring to transcendence as an epiphany where you become one with everything, where you feel you are totally connected to everything that exists. Nevertheless, we all have this deep longing to experience transcendence. It is our desire to become greater and go beyond our inner limitations, our fear, our ego, our greed, and our self-centeredness. There are sometimes moments in life that allow us to be in touch with this extraordinary part of us that is beyond our self-concerns.

You may have heard this story. I do not know if it is a true story or simply a parable. One time a man was standing with his child waiting for a train. Another man standing on the train platform had some kind of an attack and fell off of the platform. Suddenly a train approached. At that moment, the man with the child jumped onto the train tracks and covered the body of the man who had fallen with his own body to protect him. Soon the train arrived, and the man who had fallen became conscious. The other man said, "Don't get up. The train is here." This is quite an extraordinary story in one sense, but it's not really that extraordinary because everybody has this innate courage to act in such circumstances. The story reminds us that we are all spiritual, and our best impulses are selfless, heroic, and courageous, even though somehow we don't allow ourselves to be in touch with that impulse every day.

We usually feel that we are self-centered. We get lost in our fear and our worry, and we end up caring about the small things in our life. Even so, we each have this amazing heart waiting for us to recognize it. Overall there are many signs that humanity as a whole is evolving. This is very good news because we are influencing each other all of the time. We are all connected to each other on the level of consciousness, more than we can see or usually acknowledge. In our current state of human evolution, we are still very stuck with our own ego. We all have layers of unconscious habits that we need to purify eventually. There is very powerful greed and self-centeredness in the consciousness of the collective, which we can see everywhere. We are very influenced by the consciousness of the world, the society, and also the culture we are part of. That's why it is so difficult for us to go inside and be in touch with that spiritual impulse, that impulse that wants to become greater. It wants us to love, to let go of fear, and to let go of our self-centeredness.

Imagine that we lived in some kind of utopian society where everyone was quite evolved. Imagine we lived in a society where everyone was a buddha. Imagine that there were buddhas driving cars on the highways and buddhas running the restaurants. When we went into a restaurant to eat, all of the waiters would be buddhas. When we looked around, one buddha would be ordering pasta while another would be ordering something else. Some buddhas would be drinking red wine and getting a little silly. Of course, this utopia is totally in our imagination. But imagine that we were literally born into a society that was totally created with love. Imagine that we grew up in a society where everyone was a buddha, including our parents, relatives, friends, and teachers. Most probably we would all be in touch with that great impulse all of the time because we were being influenced by love rather than fear and generosity rather than greed all of the time.

It's true that throughout history we all have a longing for some kind of utopian world. When we read ancient scriptures, they often describe this human longing for a perfect, utopian society or world. In Tantric Buddhism, there is a region called Oddiyana, somewhere in India. The ruler of that kingdom was someone who became a great yogi meditator. He invited all of the citizens to meditate, and then everybody became enlightened. But this is only written in a book. Don't worry. It's not going to happen in our lifetime. It may never happen. There may never be a time when the whole human society is totally enlightened.

By the way, we don't even know what it means to be enlightened. We have a lot of concepts and ideas about it. Sometimes we have to let go of these concepts. So, when you look into your inner world you may be a little confused. You may say, "I don't see any kind of heroic or spiritual impulse inside me. All I see are bundles of fear, greed, and confusion." Yes, we have fear, greed, and confusion, but this is not who we really are. We are intrinsically spiritual. We are born at this time in human history, and we are influenced, of course, by our karmic conditions and also by the state of the collective mind, the state of the world. But when we go to a temple or to a meditation retreat, we sometimes feel and are in touch with this wonderful impulse. People do not come to meditation retreats for entertainment, or for the food, or for security. Illusions of security are not offered in meditation retreats. In fact, all notions of security are deconstructed.

I was leading a meditation retreat in Malaysia recently, and I told everybody that when we come to a meditation retreat, we should imagine that we are being welcomed to a spiritual landfill. We don't come to pick anything up. In fact, we have to drop something. We have to drop our illusions, including the illusion of security. The reason we come together is because of our spiritual impulse. This impulse awakens by itself. Then everyone comes together with this wonderful feeling that their spiritual impulse is awakening. We just sit together as a community that is in touch with their spiritual impulse. This impulse wants to wake up. It wants to let go of fear, anger, hatred, and greed. It wants to love. Therefore, many of us feel that we are in touch with something very wonderful. To some extent, we can even get attached to that feeling. We feel that we really want to be this version of ourselves. We want to be openhearted and courageous. We want to forgive everybody and let go of all of our old concerns about security, certainty, and success. We seek out centers and retreats where we feel supported and where we are influenced by the love and the awakening of everybody around us.

There is some encouraging news that humanity as a whole is evolving, that we are becoming more and more mature. We are discovering that actually we have evolved quite a lot from our past. Scientists and scholars have studied the skulls and bones of the people who lived many centuries ago. They have discovered signs of damage and trauma on the skulls and bones of most of the people. There was probably a lot of violence and war happening on a daily basis in these distant days.

Scientists and scholars have also discovered that the perimeter of our compassion and love is actually expanding. In the past people loved and experienced compassion toward a very limited number of people. Perhaps only toward their family and a few members of their tribe. Now we are living in a time when we sometimes feel love and compassion toward people who live all the way on the other side of the world, for people who have different cultural values and religions than our own. Not only do we have feelings of love and compassion, we actually take action to translate our love and compassion into helping them. Even though we may not identify ourselves as religious, we all have this natural longing to be noble. We may not have the desire to become one with the Divine or come into union with God, or whatever we might call that, the Supreme Reality, the Godhead, or Brahman. Our deep longing for transcendence comes from our desire to become great inside, to become less self-centered and more compassionate. Our longing for transcendence comes from our desire to be free from the limitations that our old consciousness constructed.

Ultimately transcendence is this powerful experience where we feel a paradigm shift happening in our consciousness. Now and then we feel so tired with our ordinary consciousness, which is filled with fear and anxiety, that we wish there would be a paradigm shift. We have a longing for this shift to happen to the extent that we see reality from a totally different view. We have a longing to experience a reality where there is no more division, where there is no more duality between ourself and others, where we become one with everything and see everything as pure and sacred. When there is no duality, there are no longer friends and no longer enemies. We can love everyone.

People have tried all sorts of methods to bring about such paradigm shifts. Some people use a ceremony to produce this radical shift in their consciousness. We can use single-pointed concentration, or mantra, or fasting, and eventually our old mind-set, our old consciousness, begins to dissolve. We feel that we are stepping into a new realm of consciousness where we feel that there is no contraction, no more pain, no more struggle. We feel that the whole world, the whole universe, is sacred, and we feel that everybody, every living being, is a buddha. This is one of the awarenesses that we try to experience when we do Tantric ceremonies if you are familiar with them. I'm a Tibetan Tantric Buddhist, and we do lots of ceremonies in order to drop our egoic mind and experience this paradigm shift where we can see that everyone is holy, everyone is sacred. Even the whole universe is sacred.

One time I had a dream. There was an animal release ceremony. There were many boxes, and each box was filled with animals that somebody wanted to rescue and release. There were many people involved. One man was shouting, "Everybody come here and pick up a box." But we didn't know what was in the box. Even in the dream, I was a Tantric Buddhist, and of course I wanted to save all of these animals because all of them are sacred. All of them are living buddhas. So I picked up a box. I didn't know what was in it. When I opened it, it was filled with cockroaches! I had never felt the kind of resistance I felt toward the cockroaches. But when I looked around, there were a lot of people watching me. I didn't want to throw the box away because it would mess up my image as a Tantric Buddhist. This is my confession. This is one of those dreams that I never forget even though it happened many years ago. Finally, I closed the box and made sure that the expression on my face didn't show any kind of resistance. I wanted to look like I was happy with all of these living buddhas. I was happy to rescue the cockroaches. Then the dream ended.

Isn't it funny how our identities—our spiritual identities or our political identities—continue to play a very active role even in our dreams. This dream happened maybe ten years ago. Hopefully I'm a little more evolved today. And yet even when we have these paradigm shifts in our consciousness through ceremonies, we can't actually stay in those experiences. They go away eventually, and we are taken over by our old mind, taken over by our old habits of fear, confusion, self-centeredness, and self-concern.

It's very liberating when we can let go of ourself for a while. We let go by transcending ourselves. This is one reason people like watching movies. When we go to the movie theater, everybody is eating their golden-colored popcorn, drinking Coca-Cola, and watching the movie. They are all happy. It's like a modern temple where everybody is experiencing transcendence. It's transcendence for at least two hours when all of our problems are forgotten. After the movie ends, they will all come back. So, that's not true transcendence; it's false transcendence.

We try to experience transcendence sometimes by the wrong means. True transcendence is actually a radical paradigm shift. It is the radical experience of going away from the state of mind that is self-centered and into the state of mind that is other-centered. Our heart knows exactly what this means. But our egoic mind says, "I don't know what you are talking about. This is a very weird reality. Going away from self-centered to other-centered? What do you mean, 'other-centered'?" But actually, our heart already knows. Have you ever experienced conflict between your heart and mind? Your heart wants to go to the infinite and become greater, and your mind wants to stay small and limited. Your heart wants to love somebody, and your mind says, "How can you love that person?" Your heart says, "I want to forgive that person." Your mind says, "You can't forgive that person because they did this and that to you." Your heart says, "Oh, this person is pure and divine. I want to experience reverence for this person." Your mind says, "How can you revere this person. This person is such and such." Mind comes with so much judgment. Our heart wants a world of peace, and our mind wants to have a conflict. That's why world peace is actually some kind of mantra we have been reciting for a long time. Politicians throw these words around all of the time, and so do musicians and activists. When you listen to music, sometimes you find this phrase "world peace." In some sense we all throw the words "world peace" around. There are institutions that will give us an award if they somehow decide that we are an individual who has been working hard for world peace. Everyone talks about world peace, but at the same time we have world violence. And this demonstrates that as humans we are not one-dimensional; we are complicated creatures.

Human beings are the most complex creatures. We are unlike animals. They are not complex. For example, dogs or cats are not complex. They are quite easygoing. They want to sleep. They want to eat. They want to be petted, and they want to love. That's pretty much it. They don't have a conflict between their higher self and their lower self. They don't have this thing called a "higher self" versus a "lower self." As human beings we have a conflict thinking that there is a lower self with the small ego and a higher self that we are going to eventually realize and be in union with. So we have a fundamental conflict between our heart and our mind. Our mind judges and criticizes things. Our mind wants to hold on to the problems. Our mind wants to divide. Our heart wants to unite, forgive, love, and surrender. Almost every human being has this wonderful heart that has a desire for peace. And then we also have this very complicated mind that wants to divide and create conflict. It is, actually, addicted to misery and pain. True transcendence is a universal experience that everybody can have access to regardless of their identity as spiritual or secular. True transcendence is going away from being self-centered and being other-centered. We don't need any religious identity to experience it. All that is required is that we have a heart. Our old reality is that there is "me," who is the center of the universe. This "me" is the most important individual in human history and in the entire galaxy. Isn't this quite a wild delusion? This "me" is the most important person. "Me's" suffering is somehow greater than anyone else's suffering. "Me's" hunger is bigger than everybody else's hunger. "Me's" problems are bigger than anyone else's, and somehow "me's" happiness is more important than anybody else's happiness. This sense of being the center of the universe and being attached to that is so painful, so contracting. It's like a little invisible prison that we have created. It's like a form of solitary confinement. There is no joy, there is no bliss, there is no freedom in that imaginary entity that we are so attached to. The stronger our attachment to this "me," the stronger the pain and suffering we experience.

The experience of being other-centered is that we come out of that invisible solitary confinement and experience this unconditional joy and freedom. We are no longer concerned with our own well-being. This does not mean that we should become a martyr and sacrifice ourselves. This is about no longer being attached to the personal self, no longer lost in our self-concerns. Actually, we are expanding our heart. We are loving everybody else the way we love ourself. We are caring for everybody else the way we care for ourself.

There are practices in the Tibetan traditions that help us experience this transcendence, this true transcendence. One practice is called equalizing oneself with others or exchanging oneself with others. The practice begins by opening our heart and recognizing the suffering of everyone. As we know there are many forms of suffering that people are going through. There is hunger, thirst, war, violence, abuse, injustice, and mental illness just to name a few. There are myriad forms of human suffering. In the practice, we don't stay self-centered; we are no longer lost in ourself. We begin to open our heart, and in our mind we feel in touch with the myriad forms of pain and suffering that all of humanity and even all living beings are experiencing. We begin to feel their pain in the same way that we feel our own pain. We begin to feel that we are the same as everybody else, and everybody else is the same as us. In some sense, we feel that we are all equal. We give up the idea that we are the most important individual in the galaxy. We feel that everybody is equally important. We feel that everybody's suffering is equally painful, and everybody's happiness is equally important.

Another practice that is often done with visualization is exchanging oneself with others. We visualize people we like—for example, our family members and friends. Then we visualize those we might call enemies. The truth is there are no enemies. No one is our enemy; enemy is simply a mental construct. There are some people who are in pain, and sometimes they are a pain in the neck. That's pretty much it. Then we visualize all of humanity. We keep expanding the perimeter of our concern by visualizing all living beings, those who have form and those who have no form. In our mind we are holding everybody and we are actually allowing ourself to take on their pain and their suffering. Then we imagine that we are giving them our own happiness, our enlightenment, our freedom, and all of our goodness. So that is a shift of our paradigm. Until a moment ago, our ego wanted everything for itself. Our ego cares only about our own needs. It cares only about our own happiness, and it wants us to be free from suffering. Our ego couldn't care less about the happiness and suffering of other people. But here we are totally changing that old paradigm. Now we care about the sorrow of others more than we care about our own sorrow.

This is of course a method, a method that allows us to experience that paradigm shift in our consciousness. And in that moment, we feel that our heart is filled with joy. We wonder, "What happened to me? I am no longer concerned about myself. I had been worrying about myself, my life. I'm afraid of my death, my illness. I'm afraid of losing my security. I want this and that. I have been feeling a bit of pride over what I have, pride over my accomplishments, my little glories. What happened to me? Now I'm no longer concerned about myself. I'm totally concerned about the well-being of other people. I'm feeling the magnitude of the suffering of others." This is a true paradigm shift, a shift that we all should be looking for.

14

countless blessings

middle-aged man I have known for decades quite often comes to my talks. He has a lot of challenges in his life that seem unending. He is one of those people who wind up having many difficulties in life. Recently, he was passing through the Bay Area and he visited me. When I asked him how he was doing, he said, "Every day is a new day." That was quite a profound response. When he said that, I felt that there was great wisdom in his heart. Just as he said, each day is also a new day for each of us. This is a perspective that we might like to hold in our hearts and our minds in order to remind ourselves that every day is a new day. Each day when we wake up, we don't know exactly what is going to happen. We don't have absolute certainty about how the day is going to unfold.

Each day can bring a lot of surprises. Some surprises can be painful. Others can be quite pleasant and wonderful. Many years ago, there was a newspaper story about a woman who was driving to work and stopped at a red light. Suddenly a man who wanted to kill himself jumped off the sixth floor of a building. He landed on her car. She got injured and had to be taken to the hospital. This is quite a dramatic story reminding us that we don't know how the day is going to unfold when we wake up. This lady probably had no idea when she was driving to work that a very unhappy man was soon going to land on her car and change her life, at least for a while.

Of course, most of the time our days are kind of ordinary. That's how we experience them. But the truth of the matter is that every day is unique and filled with many surprises, wonders, magic, and opportunities to grow if we really pay attention and if we live with an open heart. No doubt there will also be many opportunities each day that can be embraced as opportunities to grow; to become mature and evolve; and to practice love, compassion, and courage—especially if we are really interested in spiritual growth. Some of these opportunities are not soothing and comforting. But if we pay attention and if we open our heart, every day brings many wonders and opportunities to each of us to grow, mature, and become a bodhisattva, to become an awakened heroine or an awakened hero. It's not like we have to face tragedy or big challenges in order to embrace all of these events each day as an opportunity to grow and wake up. We'll find that there are many opportunities in our relationship with the world each day and in our interactions with other people.

The situations we face each day are changing constantly from one hour to the next, from one moment to the next. This is why Buddhist traditions embrace the idea of the eight worldly conditions: happiness and suffering; fame and insignificance; praise and blame; gain and loss. These eight worldly conditions, or vicissitudes, are intrinsically unpredictable, transient. They don't last for a long time. They go away and then return. As human beings somehow or other we are always experiencing these eight vicissitudes. Think of pleasure and pain. Each day we may recognize that we are experiencing the never-ending, ever-changing, ungraspable eight worldly vicissitudes such as pain and pleasure. There is physical pain and pleasure as well as emotional pain and pleasure. Maybe one moment we are experiencing pleasure, and then within a half hour we may end up experiencing either physical or emotional pain. We never know what will happen even in the next few moments. We are, indeed, experiencing these eight worldly vicissitudes all of the time. Think about praise and blame. Maybe we wake up in the morning and run into someone who says, "Oh, I love your hairstyle." In that moment we experience joy. We feel the emotions of pleasure and elation. We feel uplifted. Then somebody says that they don't like something about us. They don't like the clothes we are wearing or they don't like what we are doing. They may call us a name. People are always calling each other names, which is a very destructive thing to do to each other. We call each other names out of unawareness and unconsciousness. These simple examples show how every human being experiences these eight worldly conditions every day.

When I was young, a quite prestigious family lost their uncle and invited thirty of us to recite volumes of Buddhist scriptures as part of a ceremony dedicated to him. While we were reading these ancient scriptures, we came across many parables and stories. I remember one story that told about two monks who were traveling together through a forest. They saw two monkeys jumping around. One of the monks was athletic and extremely agile and strong. He started jumping around and even climbed one of the trees. The other monk said, "Oh, you are so agile and flexible. Just like a monkey." Later, when the less-athletic monk died, he was reborn five hundred times as a monkey. Even though he told his friend he was so agile and flex-ible, blaming somebody or calling someone a name, like "a monkey," was such a serious deed that he ended up reborn as a monkey five hundred times. Of course, we should not take that literally. The whole point of this parable is to show how destructive it is when we blame someone or criticize them or when we call other peo-ple names. One moment we might be receiving praise. Somebody praises us for our work or the clothes we are wearing. How do we feel when somebody praises us? We are uplifted and elated. How do we feel when somebody criticizes or blames us for something? We may feel sad or a bit depressed. It would be worthwhile to inquire how we feel when we experience emotional or physical pleasure and emotional or physical pain.

Then there is gain and loss. My community in California has experienced both gain and loss, especially in relation to land we have acquired in the Big Sur area. Our community acquired a very sweet piece of land with a swimming pool, a gazebo, and some lovely cabins. When we got it, we had fantasies that many of our friends would come there to visit. They would meditate and become en-lightened, and there would be swimming. There was even a Japanese sauna that they could use after swimming. When you combine all of these things together, the fantasy was amazing—enlightenment, spiritual awakening, swimming, Japanese sauna, Big Sur, and red-woods. We were all elated! After we acquired the land, I went there and stayed for one night. It was magical. I got up around midnight and went outside. I breathed clean air and felt all of the elements were alive—the sky, the water, and the land. I had a feeling of bliss, thinking that many of you would come there and meditate.

I left our retreat land, Sweetwater Sanctuary, and maybe two days after that, I received an urgent phone call reporting that there was a fire raging in the area. Within a few days the sanctuary was completely consumed by the fire. Most of the structures on the land were burned down. That was a very powerful spiritual teaching. It reminded me of the teaching on gain and loss. There are these worldly conditions, vicissitudes, and we can't hold on to them. They will go away—sometimes in a simple fashion and sometimes in a dramatic fashion. My community experienced the joy of gain—we got this beautiful retreat land. We had all of these plans and fantasies about what we were going to do. Then shortly after that, we lost this beautiful land that we were attached to. That loss sometimes comes with anxiety, fear, or maybe even pain if we are not ready to let go. The point I am trying to make is that most of the situations we go through every day are often unpredictable. We don't have absolute control over what situation might arise each day and what situation might not arise.

When we wake up each morning, we might like to remind ourselves that this is a totally new day and we don't have certainty regarding how this day is going to unfold. We also don't know who we are going to meet. Knowing this, how are our interactions with people during this day going to unfold? We may go through blame, praise, gain, or loss. Or perhaps the day is going to unfold in a series of miracles and blessings, which is true most of the time. We must remember that each day is filled with countless blessings. All we need to do sometimes is to refresh our heart and mind and let go of the grip of our inner demons, fear and anxiety. We can open our heart to see everything as a beautiful expression of this life—life that is much bigger than the ego, bigger than our personal world, bigger than our hopes and fears. Then we will notice that each day is filled with so many blessings. Then we can express our gratitude for these blessings. It all depends on the realm of consciousness that we are living in.

One time an optimist and a pessimist ran into each other on the street. They wound up having a conversation. The optimist, with great joy, said, "Did you know that we are living in the best of all possible worlds?" The pessimist sat for a while with a grim expression on his face. Then said, "I'm afraid that is true." We can allow ourselves to be like this pessimist and let all of our inner demons, the demons of fear, anxiety, and agitation, completely run our mind and heart. Then we feel that somehow, we are struggling every day. We feel like our experience with the universe is based on struggle, not based on harmony, not based on love. But if we become like that optimist by opening our heart to life each day, then we welcome all of these blessings.

This is not just abstract thinking; this is true. Every day is filled with many blessings. One of my favorite ceremonies is the blessing of food, which many people don't do in modern culture. In many ancient cultural traditions, people performed the ceremony of blessing their food all of the time. Some blessings can have a very religious connotation, but the blessing of food does not have to have a religious overtone. It can just be a simple ceremony. When we drink tea or coffee or when we sit down to eat, we can pause for a while and do our own improvisational ceremony. We can say whatever comes spontaneously to our heart. We can thank the universe for giving us the food on the table. We can also be thankful to everybody whose work brought us this meal. We can be extremely thankful for the fact that we are not hungry, that we have something to eat. Many, many people in our world are struggling and not finding food. They don't know whether or not they will have anything to eat this evening. They don't know how they are going to feed their beautiful children.

We might like to start each day by bringing about bodhicitta, the awakened heart. Bodhicitta is a Buddhist concept, but it is not exclusively Buddhist. Bodhicitta is much bigger than Buddhism. Bodhicitta is a universal spirituality. The awakened heart is a human spirituality. One doesn't have to be Buddhist to experience this universal heart. This is the most profound human experience that we can have, bodhicitta, the awakened heart. There are a lot of complicated theories and many ways of explaining bodhicitta, the awakened heart, which we don't have to get into. A Tibetan lama who is a friend of mine recently said, "We Tibetans have a special gift of making simple things very complicated." That was a very wise statement. It makes sense. In the Tibetan Buddhist tradition, we have a lot of texts and scriptures. We study them and debate them. He's right. I don't know if it is a gift or not, but we do have a cultural tendency to make simple things really complicated. Then people think that it must be really profound because they can't understand it.

Bodhicitta is truly simple. Let's cut through all of the theoretical doctrine. The human heart is very simple. It's all about our willingness to open our heart to life and to all expressions of life. It means that we are holding an aspiration and commitment, not to anybody but to ourself. We are committed to living each day fully, and we are not going to live with fear, anger, or resistance. We are going to be completely ready to welcome everything, including the eight worldly vicissitudes. We are going to welcome the unpleasant as well as the pleasant meetings with people whoever they might be. It may be our aunt who is visiting from out of town. Or perhaps our future soul mate is going to have dinner with us. The point is to hold this intention, this gut-level aspiration that we are going to open our heart to everything, all of the situations that challenge or comfort us as an expression of life. We hold the intention to respond to each of them with love, courage, and an open heart rather than from our old habitual patterns, which can sometimes be aggression, anger, fear, resistance, mistrust, or judgment. We hold the intention not to defend or even to offend.

Early in the morning, when we wake up, seems to be a very important moment. I grew up in a culture where most people had the belief that when the sun shines and reflects inside your house, it is the most magical and sacred moment in the day. My people are a little superstitious. They never loved the sunset. They thought the sunset was the sun for the dead. They were even a little bit afraid of looking at the sunset, but they loved the morning, especially when the sun was rising. That was the time for them to recite prayers. Just like that there are moments each day that can be very special and have perhaps some kind of spiritual meaning. My understanding is that when you wake up in the early morning, that is the moment you can take as the most important, most sacred, and holiest moment, whatever that means. So, in that moment that you wake up, the very first thing you want to do is invite bodhicitta.

Wouldn't it be amazing if we started every morning by waking up and developing this habit that the first thought, the first feeling, the first impulse we bring to our house of consciousness is not our fear, not our worry, not our anxiety, not thoughts about our first cup of coffee or the weather or the traffic. Rather, the first thought that we invite into the house of our consciousness is to develop bodhicitta, the awakened heart. This awakened heart is not about Buddhism in the ultimate sense. It is taught in Buddhism, but it not a Buddhist thing. It is a human spirituality. So, imagine that we wake up every morning and the first thought that we invite into the house of our consciousness is bodhicitta. This aspiration. This gut-level aspiration of self-love, self-commitment with the thought that today is a new day. In this new day we will have the willingness to let go of all of our expectations and preferences. We will have the willingness to meet all of life's situations with an open heart. We will meet the eight worldly conditions, but we don't know exactly which ones we are going to meet. Nevertheless, we will meet all of them with an open heart, with courage, and we vow not to respond to them from our old egoic habits. Then every day becomes a day filled with many blessings. Every day becomes an inward spiritual journey. Every day becomes the dharma, the path to inner awakening, the path to inner liberation.

15

the ultimate awakening

In late January or early February many people celebrate the anniversary of Longchenpa, a very well-known Dzogchen master in the Tibetan tradition who lived in the fourteenth century. He is someone who really epitomized and embodied the profound, brilliant wisdom of the Tibetan spiritual tradition. As you know my country, Tibet, is a very spiritual country that has both preserved priceless Buddhist traditions including Vajrayana, or Tantric Buddhism, and also developed a whole new body of spiritual wisdom and practices. In many ways, we could say that Tibetan people are quite spiritual. Starting in the 1960s, and even in the 1990s through today, people in the West had this fantasy, this projection, that all Tibetan people were spiritually enlightened.

In the 1990s somebody brought me video cassettes of the *Star Wars* movies. They said, "Watch them. It's a good way to learn English." I was surprised in one episode, when these very cute Ewoks suddenly appeared and started speaking Tibetan. "How are you? What time is it?" I started wondering why they put Tibetan language in the film. Maybe they thought that the Tibetans were a very kind and unusual people. We are kind but not always as adorable as those Ewoks. Tibetans have all of the human neuroses that everybody else has—ego, fear, and so forth. Nevertheless, the Tibetan adepts left very wonderful wisdom legacies that can benefit all humanity. For example, Longchenpa's writings talked about the idea that all circumstances, all of life's conditions may appear friendly to oneself. The idea is that we can actually practice a certain set of attitudes and perspectives or even radically change our outlook in relationship to life and reality. In other words, we can learn to turn our consciousness upside down. If we can do that, then we can see that all circumstances can appear friendly in our experience. All circumstances—not just the pleasant and favorable ones but even the difficult ones that might be very painful and traumatizing like loss, separation, death, death of our loved ones, loss of our fortune and our health—can appear friendly.

Perhaps we are struggling with difficult situations in our life, whatever they are. Today we are dealing with one difficulty that may eventually resolve itself. Then we have time to celebrate, thinking that now we have overcome all of the difficulties in our life. But sooner or later, life gives us another gift that is not always pleasant. Then we have another difficulty, another challenging or painful situation that we need to confront. Many of us feel that we are always kind of struggling with this human life. We feel that we are always coming up against challenges. Sometimes the challenges are big, like health or family issues, and then there are small challenges all of the time. Maybe we don't like the weather today or we suddenly get a flat tire while we are driving on the highway. Yet all of the conditions in our life are intrinsically impermanent; they will not last forever.

The difficult ones will not last forever. In the same way, even the conditions we like, the ones that comfort us, will not last forever. Therefore we always have to be ready to let go of our attachment to our conditions. We have to let go of the ones that comfort us and give us happiness and a sense of security because they are bound to change sooner or later. There are also conditions that don't go away easily, like chronic illness. Yet we can always change the state of our own mind, our perspective, and our attitude in relationship to almost every circumstance that we go through, even the difficult ones that may stay with us for a long time.

Recently someone wrote to me to request that I spend time with someone in our community who was having suicidal thoughts. I met with this young person in their twenties or thirties, very bright and intelligent. She felt like she was very fortunate and had many blessings in her life, but she was also having suicidal thoughts. She said she had a feeling that she had made a huge mistake in life. I invited her to go inside and inquire and find the root of her suicidal thought. Of course, I encouraged her to reach out and get all of the help she could get from people, including spiritual friends, relatives, and professionals. I also told her that she needed to have faith in herself and also in life. "If you just have faith in your own life, in your strength and your power and your capacity to overcome this, some day you may actually be living in a very different state of mind where you don't see all of these obstacles in your life. You may even experience a sense of joy and meaning in your life." Basically, I said, "Just wait. Can you just wait a little bit? We don't know exactly what will happen. Conditions may change or they may not change, but the state of your consciousness changes.

And the state of your consciousness can be changed." Then I gave her this analogy. Imagine that you traveled all the way to a distant land, maybe Iceland, Norway, or Alaska, to catch the magical sight of the Northern Lights. Then you became very impatient. Maybe you had to wait just a half an hour longer. But you said, "Oh, I have already been here for three hours. I am leaving now." Then we both started laughing. Humor is always good. Maybe that was a good analogy, maybe not, but the idea is that we have to wait a little bit. I told her, "We just have to wait a little bit. Some day you are going to wake up, and you'll be able to come out of this inner darkness. You'll see goodness and beauty in this life. But you need to wait for a while. Have trust and faith in yourself and continue to be positive and hopeful."

All conditions are actually changing most of the time. One moment we are very healthy, or maybe we fall in love. Then one day we discover that we are not very healthy, or maybe we fall out of love. These things happen all of the time. One moment we are young and healthy, the next moment we look into the mirror and see that we are aging. We wonder, "How did this happen? I thought I was very young, but the mirror doesn't lie." The mirror can be very heartless. It points out our aging process with direct honesty. I remember when I was learning English and came across the word *mortified*. The sentence that went with it said, "She was mortified to discover wrinkles on her forehead."

Even the existence that we are enjoying right now is not permanent. This body is not permanent. Sooner or later it will collapse. That doesn't mean we always have to be scared and fearful because everything is going to change sooner or later. Instead we should learn how to open our heart to all expressions of life, including the ever-changing nature of conditions. We should celebrate everything that happens in our life, even the painful things, if we can.

The Thai Buddhist master Ajahn Chah was so revered that when he died, about a million people came to pay their respect to his work and his legacy. Even the Thai royal family came. One time, when he was alive, somebody brought him a gift of an expensive antique cup. It was supposed to have been made in China during the Ming dynasty. He picked up the cup in front of everybody and said, "This cup is already broken." Because it is already broken, we can let go of our attachment to it in case someday it breaks, which it will. At the same time, we can enjoy it, and we can enjoy drinking from it. In many ways, everything is already broken. We are all broken. This whole world is broken. When we look around, we cannot find anything that is not broken. Even if we spend the whole day trying to find something that is not broken, in the end we will not find anything that is not intrinsically broken. We are all broken, unbroken too. Everything we are all enjoying right now is already broken. This planet is broken. And because everything is broken, because everything is eventually going to dissolve and fall apart, then maybe we can let go of our unhealthy attachment to things but also enjoy everything. Enjoy what we have. Enjoy all of the conditions that arise in our life with an open heart.

Learning how to experience that all conditions can appear to be friendly to us is related to our ability to shift our consciousness. We can literally almost turn it upside down so that we look at the whole of reality from a new point of view, a point of view that is completely different from the one we are familiar with. Maybe someday we can be so liberated inside that we can open our heart no matter what happens. Someday maybe we'll be playing music and dancing ecstatically in the streets. Our neighbor may come out and ask why we are dancing so ecstatically. We might say, "I just learned that I lost all of my money." Of course, it is almost unimaginable, but it's possible. Ancient mystics were able to turn their consciousness completely upside down. They were able to look at the whole of reality from another mind, another point of view. They were able to open their hearts and embrace everything that happened as some kind of expression of reality that is much bigger than their personal preferences, their personal choices and desires, and their likes and dislikes.

One of my friends was reading the teachings of another extraordinary Tibetan mystic and mahasiddha, Patrul Rinpoche, who lived in the nineteenth century. My friend related that Patrul Rinpoche said everything that we think is bad, to him is good. Everything that we think is good, to him is bad. He also talked about actually inviting difficulties and hardships. Some of the Tibetan masters didn't pray for longevity, success, or money. They actually prayed intentionally for challenges and difficulties. Can you believe how unconventional that is? Maybe they were praying for problems so they could embrace the challenges as a heroic opportunity to transcend their self-centeredness, their preferences, and to learn how to grow inside, to learn how to become truly openhearted, courageous, and selfless. Perhaps they used those difficult circumstances as an opportunity to experience the ultimate awakening, which is going beyond all hope and fear. We too can practice turning our consciousness upside down by trying to see what people think is bad as good. There are many perspectives we can practice to help us completely change our paradigm of reality.

Recently somebody asked me if I would talk about the law of attraction. I don't know much about this, but perhaps many of you are familiar with it. I did some research on this idea. It turns out that maybe this idea of the law of attraction is in contradiction with or even kind of an opposite position from the spiritual path that I have been following. The spiritual path in the Buddhist tradition is not really about working with our heart and mind and intentionally trying to have all of our desires met. It is not about trying to manifest money, success, a relationship, good health, and so forth in our consciousness. It's actually the direct opposite of that. The path I follow is about turning our consciousness upside down. It is a path of trying to see all of our difficulties as opportunities. All of life's difficulties can be a blessing. Conditions like not having money can be a blessing. Not having great success can be a blessing. Of course, you have to go out in the world and make a living so you can take care of yourself. But spending hours and hours on the meditation cushion trying to magnetize all of these earthly glories is kind of missing the point. The spiritual path is not really about that. It is about learning how to open our heart and have compassion. It is about not losing our dignity and finding true fulfillment whether we have worldly fortune or not. It is about our ability, to a certain extent, to go beyond all conditions and stay openhearted and dignified.

One time I lived at a lovely Buddhist meditation center in the Santa Cruz mountains. It was a very beautiful center, a wonderful community, and I really enjoyed living there. But there was a lady who stayed near me, and every early morning I heard her crying. Usually she cried after her morning practice in which she recited all of these beautiful prayers and chants in Tibetan. I thought that she was crying because she was in love with the spiritual path or that she was crying out of compassion. Then one day she said, "I am crying because I need a boyfriend. Could you give me a mantra that I can use to manifest a boyfriend?" I said, "So sorry, I don't have any such mantra." There are no mantras that help anybody manifest wealth, prosperity, or any of the favorable circumstances. Mantras are not for reifying and solidifying our self-centered desires and our wants. Mantras are reminders for developing love, compassion, and awareness.

There are two ways or methods that we can use in our everyday life to experience what Longchenpa and other Tibetan teachers were trying to express—two methods for experiencing this very profound spiritual experience or whatever you would like to call it. One is learning how to change our perspective, and the other is learning how to surrender. Changing our perspective is basically changing our fundamental philosophy, our fundamental view about life and reality. We literally turn our consciousness upside down to the extent that what we have seen as unfavorable or negative, suddenly we see as potentially positive. Illness, separation, and loss—which we usually consider unfortunate and unfavorable conditions, things that we try to get rid of or try to run away from—suddenly turn into blessings. We can think, "This is kind of a blessing from somewhere, maybe from life or from the universe, because I can use this pain, I can use this illness, this separation, this loss to learn how to grow. I can go inside and learn how to practice nonattachment and letting go. Maybe I can even find this thing called unconditional happiness, happiness that is not dependent on external causes and conditions."

Many great teachers and masters, including Buddha, talked about unconditional happiness. Buddha said there are two kinds of happiness: temporary happiness and unconditioned happiness. *Unconditioned happiness* is the happiness that arises from your awakened consciousness. It is not contingent on any external conditions. Or we could say that we are going to embrace this suffering, this pain so that we can have a greater understanding of the pain and suffering that other people go through. Now and then we run into people, loved ones, or friends who talk about their physical pain. Yet unless we have experienced physical pain in our own lives, we really don't completely know what it means to be in physical pain. We may have some kind of intellectual or mental sympathy or compassion, but we may not be able to open our heart completely and really acknowledge the physical pain that somebody else is going through. But if we take our own physical pain as a blessing rather than some unfavorable negativity, then we can use it as an amazing spiritual path through which we can develop compassion toward others. There are stories of people who were trying to be free inside, totally liberated by practicing meditation. It didn't work and then somehow a host of misfortunes struck them. They lost everything, and that forced them to be completely liberated inside and thus to be truly happy. Perhaps the next time we are dancing and singing songs will be because we got a big promotion, or perhaps we won the lottery. But maybe it's because we lost everything, and that's why we are dancing and singing songs in bliss.

Another method we can try in order to experience this very profound liberation in which all conditions appear friendly is through surrendering. We surrender to the way things are. We surrender to all situations. This is not about being totally passive. It's about knowing deep down inside that we actually have very little control over our own existence. Fundamentally, the idea that "my life is my show" turned out to be a delusion. It turns out that my life is actually somebody else's show. It's rather devastating news to wake up and realize that "my life is not my show." We usually think that although the entire universe may not be my show, at least my life is my show. We think that we are some kind of cosmic, karmic agent who created our life and therefore we should have 100 percent control over our life. Yet it turns out that my life is somebody else's show. We don't know who that person or that thing is. The best course is not to name it. However, if we really want to name it, we could say it is the show of the divine, a cosmic lila, or divine play. We just happen to be part of this dance, and that's why everything that happens in our life is part of the cosmic dance, the divine play. We have very little influence over what happens in our life; it's just part of the divine show. If we are Buddhist, we may say that this is a display of the great emptiness. If we are not Buddhist, we might say that this is the play of the great mystery. Whatever we say, the truth is that we don't have absolute control over our existence.

Life itself has already demonstrated that we have never had 100 percent control over our existence, including the very first stage of our existence, our birth. We are not sitting some place looking at a map and choosing where we should be born. We are not choosing our parents. Unfortunately, many people feel that they have chosen the wrong parents. The truth is there are no right parents. We don't know how long we are going to live on this planet. This is just reminding us that we never, in the first place, had absolute control over our existence. Please remember that not having control is not about giving up all of our responsibility for our life because the universe is going to take care of everything. Not having control is not being inactive. It is about knowing deep down that we are not in complete control and about knowing deep down that we should open our heart and learn not to react to disappointment with anger, resistance, and confusion.

Life is not always in accordance with our expectations and desires. Our expectations and desires are very much part of our ego structure. We can work to change our perception so we see all conditions in life as blessings. Surrendering is giving up the delusion that we are in control or the desire to be in control of everything. In addition, mantra recitation is another wonderful practice. We can memorize a sacred phrase composed by one of the great mahasiddhas or poets of the past that reminds us to surrender. Or we can compose our own phrase and turn that into a mantra or sacred phrase. I often compose a sacred phrase and then try to use it throughout the day. One of these is, "I surrender to the way things are." As a human being we know when we are not surrendering to the way things are. We know when we are resisting the way things are. We feel it in our body. We feel our whole system beginning to contract. We are reacting to life. When I recite the phrase, "I surrender to the way things are," my consciousness shifts. This beautiful phrase reminds me that I am not in control. It helps me to surrender and shift from being contracted to being more expansive, more joyful, and in a happier state of consciousness.

Dharmata Foundation carries the current inventory of Anam Thubten's books and recorded teachings through their online bookstore.

Anam Thubten travels widely to teach and conduct meditation retreats in many locations across the US and abroad. For more information, a schedule of Dharmata events, and access to the bookstore, please visit:

www.dharmata.org

Other inquries may be directed to:

info@dharmata.org

Dharmata Foundation
235 Washington Avenue
Point Richmond, California 94801

about the author

Anam Thubten grew up in Tibet and at an early age began to practice in the Nyingma tradition of Tibetan Buddhism. He is the founder and spiritual advisor of the Dharmata Foundation, and he teaches widely in the United States and internationally. He is the author of *No Self, No Problem*; *The Magic of Awareness*; and *Embracing Each Moment*.

To view Anam Thubten's teaching and retreat schedule, please visit www.dharmata.org.